New Religious Movements in Europe

RENNER Studies on New Religions

RENNER Studies on New Religions is an initiative supported by the Danish Research Council for the Humanities. The series was established to publish books on new religions and alternative spiritual movements from a wide range of perspectives. It will include works of original theory, empirical research, and edited collections that address current topics, but will generally focus on the situation in Europe.

The books will appeal to an international readership of scholars, students, and professionals in the study of religion, theology, the arts, and the social sciences. And it is hoped that this series will provide a proper context for scientific exchange between these often competing disciplines.

NEW RELIGIOUS MOVEMENTS IN EUROPE

Edited by Helle Meldgaard
& Johannes Aagaard

AARHUS UNIVERSITY PRESS

Copyright: Aarhus University Press, 1997
Printed in England by Cambridge University Press
ISBN 87 7288 548 3

Published with the financial support of the Danish Research Council for
the Humanities and the Aarhus University Research Foundation.

AARHUS UNIVERSITY PRESS
University of Aarhus
DK-8000 Aarhus C
Fax (+ 45) 8619 8433

73 Lime Walk
Headington, Oxford OX3 7AD
Fax (+ 44) 1865 750 079

Box 511
Oakville, Conn. 06779
Fax (+ 1) 860 945 9468

ANSI/NISO
Z39.48-1992

Preface

The terminology varies. Some call them religions, some call them expressions of spirituality. We call them *new religious movements*, thereby simply indicating, that these phenomena are *new* in the sense of timing, even if they have older roots, *religious* in their pretensions and practices, *movements* since most of them have not — yet — settled down as regular religions and institutions.

The new religious movements however are not so *new* as most people assume. In fact many of them are mainly new in the sense of *modern*, for they are often children of modernism, even if they may stand for 'the old paths'. And their *religiousness* is often questioned by their efficient and secular approaches to power and finances. The quality of *movements* of course depend on their ability to move, and in fact a number of them change quite a bit from decade to decade, while others continue with 'business as usual'.

Europe and North America are normally considered the typical and major areas of the new religious movements, but with some important differences since the geo-spiritual bases are quite different in those two continents.

This volume only deals with Western Europe, but we plan to edit a second volume in which the new religious movements in Central and Eastern Europe will be dealt with.

We are not perfect, for some areas are missing, and in a possible second edition we shall hopefully include the missing countries.

We publish this volume as a comprehensive and hopefully fair approach to the presentation of a manifold and ambiguous situation. We include authors of different persuasions and quite different methodological presuppositions. That means that the volume is lacking in uniformity, but at the same time it presents a variety of interpretations which hopefully will contribute to the quality of the understanding.

The volume started back in 1990 when, in Lugano, Switzerland a seminar on 'New Religious Movements: The European situation' took place, sponsored by CESNUR (Centre for Studies on New Religions. President: Monsignor Giuseppe Casale, Archbishop of Foggia, Italy) and the Swiss National Fund for Scientific Research.

This first stage was the starter, and much appreciation is due to the people in charge at that time (Jean-François Mayer and Massimo Introvigne) for their willingness to cooperate and for their thoughtful inspiration.

Aarhus, May, 1997   Helle Meldgaard
                                                        Johannes Aagaard

Contents

The Dispersion of Unorthodox Religiosity in Western Europe: A Brief Empirical Survey

Ole Riis

A few centuries ago the pastor was the major intellectual in a community of semi-literate workers or peasants. Popular beliefs, which deviated from the official model of religion, could be written off by the enlightened clergyman as surviving superstitions or as naive constructs. Local religious views could be maintained as self-affirmative traditions. The established world views could be taken for granted and supported by the local pastor. This has totally changed now.

Due to the post-industrial division of labour, higher education has become a general qualification. Many members are qualified to engage in debates on the fundamental questions concerning the meaning of life and death. Due to modern means of transportation and communication, the horizon has been expanded beyond the borders of the parish. The pastor cannot simply refer to local wisdom or to an academic status. The pastor has challengers and competitors, who cannot easily be brushed off. In many cases, the training of the pastors still follows an educational scheme, established during the era of local monopoly. Therefore, many pastors are not trained to engage in serious dialogue with those who argue consistently for deviating world views. It is understandable that some pastors withdraw from such annoying confrontations, and retract to the dwindling core-group, which still cling to the local tradition as an unquestionable truth.

The purpose of this paper is to examine the dispersion of those world views, which deviate from the official dogma of the churches.

Religious views cannot be 'measured' in any exact sense. We may, however, find indicators about what modern people believe in. These indicators tend to belong to two extreme forms. On the one hand, we may have profound expressions of serious, individual beliefs. It is, however, very difficult to find general themes and patterns in a multitude of personal statements or in-depth interviews. On the other hand, we may get a simple overview by using standardized questionnaires. Such an approach brings simple results, which are easy to interpret, but which are also simplified and shallow. The scientific venture of studying popular beliefs has to cross between the Scylla of drowning in a wealth of data and the Charybdis of skating over the thin ice of data, without noticing the currents underneath it.

It is tempting to regard popular beliefs as deviations from official religion. Several surveys have demonstrated how a decreasing proportion of West-Europeans express beliefs in the Christian creed. This does not necessarily imply that modern Europeans are secularized in the sense that they refuse to believe in a supernatural power. They may be secularized in the sense that their beliefs are privatized, questioning the tenets of the old wisdom, and relying upon a world view which they have chosen and partially made by themselves.

In order to test these interpretations, it is necessary to find indicators of non-official expressions of religion. However, non-official religion includes an assortment of heterogeneous and changeable beliefs. Most items of non-official belief are only accepted by a minority. The impact of non-official beliefs is only revealed when many items are added up. An attitude should preferably be measured by combining several questions (items) which refer to the same theme. Regrettably, such attitude scales are seldom available in cross-national studies concerning religion in the non-official mode. These problems may explain why the wealth of theories concerning private or implicit religion has not been followed up by empirical tests via survey studies.[1]

However, a few items have been used, which may illustrate the issue at hand. These regard two tenets, which are widespread enough to become part of the modern 'popular religion', namely belief in reincarnation and in astrology. Neither of these beliefs are compatible with the official interpretation of Christian dogma. They have been discussed seriously by learned theologians, and discarded as deviant beliefs during the Renaissance. The cases against Giordano Bruno and Campanella concerned belief in reincarnation and astrology. Making such beliefs anathema was not limited to the Roman Catholic church. Calvin forwarded a corresponding opinion, and underlined its consequences in the case against Servetus.

Astrology

The data concerning astrology is provided by the Eurobarometer. This series of surveys is financed by the EU, and therefore only includes member countries. The question asks whether one regards astrology as scientific. The first observation is that the proportion of 'don't know'-answers is reasonably low in most countries, but quite high in Ireland, Greece, Spain and Portugal. This seems to indicate that many people in these countries are unaware of the meaning of astrology.

In Western Europe a majority concedes that astrology is scientific. 16% of all respondents answered 'very scientific' and 40% 'sort of scientific', whereas only 29% deny such a claim. The proportion, which regards astrology as 'very scientific' is higher in Spain, Portugal, Ireland, and Greece than in the other EU-countries. Simultaneously, a high proportion in these countries find it difficult to answer the question. Scepticism towards astrology is most prominent in Italy, the United Kingdom and Belgium. Belief in astrology is thus more widespread in the poorer Roman Catholic countries, whereas scepticism is marked among the more affluent Roman Catholic countries.

Astrology may form a part of a religious world view, though it does not constitute one by itself. Astrology is intertwined with Eastern religions, as well as with European Renaissance mysticism. Ascribing astrology with a scientific status demonstrates a general confusion about the defining characteristics of modern science. It does not necessarily indicate a wholesale acceptance of a mystical cosmology.

Another international survey, the International Social Survey Programme, approached the same theme in 1991 by asking whether people agree that 'A person's star sign at birth, or horoscope, can affect the course of its future'. The survey only covers a few West European countries. In West Germany, 6% answered 'definitely true' and 22% 'probably true', 24% 'probably not true', and 36% 'definitely not true', while the remainder were undecided. In Great Britain 4% answered 'definitely true' and 24% 'probably true', 35% 'probably not true' and 28% 'definitely not true', and the rest 'don't know'. This implies that only few people

Table 1: Belief in Astrology in the EU countries

Row %	Don't know	Very scien-tific	Sort of scien-tific	Not at all scien-tific	Total
France 1	8.0	11.4	50.1	30.5	991
Belgium 2	14.6	12.7	37.8	34.9	1002
Netherlands 3	11.5	11.4	46.3	30.8	996
Germany 4	14.3	8.2	45.7	31.8	1041
Italy 5	14.7	11.7	34.1	39.5	1022
Luxembourg 6	5.9	11.6	50.2	32.3	303
Denmark 7	14.7	12.8	48.2	24.2	996
Ireland 8	21.3	18.1	34.0	26.6	1006
United Kingdom 9	7.4	15.5	37.7	39.4	1310
Greece 10	22.1	17.9	34.6	25.4	1000
Spain 11	20.5	29.5	34.3	15.7	1003
Portugal 12	27.1	29.1	29.2	14.6	1000 8.6
Column Total	1813 15.5	1873 16.0	4610 39.5	33741 28.9	1670 100.0

Source: Eurobarometer 31, 1989

in modern West European countries have world views where horoscopes form an important element. However, a sizeable proportion of modern West Europeans are open to the possibility that the star sign may affect the course of a persons life.

Corresponding figures resulted from posing questions about fortune-tellers, faith healers, or good luck charms. 5% of West Germans questioned stated that it is definitely true that 'good luck charms sometimes bring good luck', against 3% of Britons. However, 6% of West Germans say it is definitely true that 'some fortune-tellers really can foresee the future', and the figure is the same among Britons. Only 7% of West Germans find it definitely true that 'some faith healers really do have God-given healing powers', against 9% of Britons. These figures stress that despite the cultural dominance of rationalism for more than a century, a sizeable minority in modern West European countries believe in alternative ways. The pluralism of modern society opens for a wide range of alternative views, and some of these go against some of the premises of rationalism.

Reincarnation

Another comparative survey study has been organized by the European Values Survey Study. This project includes most of the West European countries. It contains several religious items, since the originators were concerned with secularization and moral changes in Western Europe. Only one of the religious items could be seen as expressing a deviation from the Christian dogma, namely belief in reincarnation. This opinion forms a more serious challenge to Christian theology.

The survey has been conducted in two rounds. The first took place around 1981 and the second in 1990-91. We are therefore able to trace changes in the opinions. A methodological comment must be made before a further analysis of the results. 'Reincarnation' was not a common term in 1981, and had to be interpreted into several languages. The Norwegian interpreters misunderstood the issue. Therefore, the term was translated into resurrection. In 1990, resurrection was explicitly separated from reincarnation in the questionnaire, and therefore the Norwegian translation was then corrected. Because of this, the Norwegian 1981-data will be excluded from further analyses. The proportion of 'don't know' answers is generally high, 21% in 1981 and 18% in 1990. In 1981, more than a fifth of the Belgians, Spaniards, Italians, Dutch and West Germans could not answer the question. In 1990 it is only in West Germany and Spain that more than a fifth answered 'don't know'. The following table shows the proportion of respondents who say 'yes' to the question in relation to all respondents, including those who say 'don't know' to the question.

Table 2: Belief in reincarnation in 11 West European Countries.

% believing in reincarnation	1981	1990
France	22	23
Britain	27	25
W. Germany	19	19
Italy	20	22
Spain	25	21
Netherlands	10	15
Belgium	13	14
Denmark	11	14
Norway	?	13
Sweden	15	16
R. of Ireland	26	18

Contrary to the general expectations concerning the expansion of unorthodox beliefs, the results show a stable level of belief in reincarnation during the 1980s. Both in 1981 and 1990, 21% of the adult population in Western Europe expressed belief in reincarnation.

If belief in reincarnation marked a conscious deviation from the dogma of the churches, then reincarnation should be more widespread among those who do not belong to any church. In fact, the tendency is quite the opposite. Relatively few, 16% of those who stand outside any church believe in reincarnation. Among members of the Roman Catholic church 21% believed in reincarnation, compared with 19% among the Protestant denominations, such as Lutheran, Calvinist or Methodist churches, and 19% among the free churches, such as Jehovah's Witnesses or the Mormons. It is hardly surprising that most Hindus and Buddhists in Western Europe believe in reincarnation. It is more problematic that about a quarter of Muslims answered this question affirmatively. This fact hints at translation errors.

Unorthodox beliefs are often associated with youth, and the unorthodox believers are often seen as influenced by 'youth religions'. However, this general impression has to be modified if belief in reincarnation is a valid indicator. The variation across generations is very moderate. Differences between men and women is much more important on this issue. More women than men believe in reincarnation. The highest proportion is found among young and middle-aged women. The figures in Table 3 are based on a combination of all the above-mentioned nations, where the relative size of the populations is taken into account:

Table 3. Belief in reincarnation in Western Europe 1990, divided into generations and age groups

% who believe in reincarnation	Men	Women
18-24 years	19	26
25-34	16	23
35-44	16	22
45-54	15	22
55-64	16	20
65-80	17	20

People in some job sectors seem especially likely to believe in reincarnation. The proportion is somewhat higher among unskilled manual workers or the unemployed. These are also sectors, where people typically have a low degree of formal education. Accordingly, the picture of a typical believer in reincarnation as a young, rather well-educated young man, has to be exchanged for a younger, less educated woman in a low-paid job.

Bricolage — a mixture of beliefs?

Belief in Heaven is quite orthodox for Christians as well as Jews and Muslims, though the interpretation of 'Heaven' may vary. In 1990, 40% of all West Europeans declared a belief in Heaven. About three quarters of all members of the non-conformist churches believe in Heaven, versus a half of all Roman Catholics and two out of five members of the mainline Protestant churches. Whereas belief in Heaven in the normal sense should hardly overlap with belief in reincarnation, there was in fact a high proportion, who affirm both beliefs, 14% in 1990. 20% expressed belief in Heaven only, and 7% in reincarnation though not in Heaven. The final 59% denied beliefs in either, or answered 'don't know'. Heaven and reincarnation may be theologically compatible through specific interpretations of the terms. This may explain why a large proportion of the European Hindus believe in both. It is, however, hardly the Indian interpretation of Heaven which has spread in Europe. The overlap between the two beliefs can be seen as an expression of a diffuse, syncretistic way of interpreting life after death.

This point may be illustrated further by the amount of overlapping between beliefs in reincarnation and resurrection. 32% of all the West European respondents confirmed belief in re-surrection. Despite the theological contradictions, 14% expressed a belief in both reincarnation and resurrection, 14% in resurrection only, and 6% in reincarnation only.

Most of those who express a belief in reincarnation also believe in one or more dogma about death affiliated with Christianity, such as belief in resurrection, Hell or Heaven. Only 4% believe in none of these Christian dogmas while they believe in reincar-nation. This implies that reincarnation in its Hindu or Buddhist variety is accepted by very few Western Europeans.

The overlapping between diverging beliefs concerning life after death indicates a general uncertainty about how to express the expectations about life after death. In some cases it may point to a misunderstanding, in others it indicates openness to a range of possible interpretations of death. This openness covers a wide range of reflections. They may on the one hand be seen as naive and muddled and on the other as highly sophisticated. The fact that most people do not fit into the theological categories does not indicate a mass conversion to Hinduism or New Age thought in

Western Europe. We still need to follow up these surveys with a wide range of in-depth interviews. However, the response pattern points to a widespread vague optimistic hope that life somehow continues after death, and some difficulties in using the theological concepts for describing this hope.

Modern religiosity is less bound to traditional authorities, and more a matter of private choice and a personal interpretation of life.[2] This type of implicit religiosity seems confused and inconsistent. This is partially due to a lack of proper instruments of measurement, and partially due to the open, pluralistic characteristics of implicit religion. The present state seems to be transitory. Implicit religion is open to new impulses and new interpretations, which may seem to provide a consistent meaning for life. Many modern Europeans seem to continue with inconsistent belief systems. These may erupt as they are challenged by the ancient questions about sufferings and risks in life. It is very difficult to predict the outcome of the present, unstable situation, also because the outcome is dependent on whether the churches realize the situation and take up the challenges.

Notes

1. For a further comment see O. Riis, *Metoder og teorier i religions-sociologien*, Aarhus: Aarhus University Press, 1996.
2. See: O. Riis, 'The Role of Religion in Legitimating the Modern Structure of Society', *Acta Sociologica* 32 (2), 1989.

CHAPTER 2

European Receptivity to the New Religions

J. Gordon Melton

Since its founding in 1969, the self-assigned task of the Institute for the Study of American Religion has been to document the growing number of different religious groups in the United States and grasp the meaning of the quantum leap in religious pluralism which has become the great fact of American religious life. However, during the past two years, we altered our research programme to concentrate our attention on Europe. This new focus has finally borne fruit in the form of three very exhaustive directories of European religions compiled by our research director Gary L. Ward. The directories, compiled using the methodologies which we had developed in our North American research, have yielded a rather dramatic overview of the European religious scene and of a very real pluralism which not only rivals but may actually surpass that in North America.

Our approach to Europe grew out of the Institute's rather unique position. The initial research which led to the founding of the Institute occurred in the 1960s and hence took place before either the creation of the new religions centre in Berkeley and the cult wars of the mid-1970s. As a result, we approached the problem of what has come to be called 'new religions' somewhat differently. Rather than focusing specifically on the narrow band of new young-adult oriented religions, we were more broadly trying to discern the meaning of the patterns of a perceived new level of religious pluralism in America and asking where it was taking us.

Because of the lack of documentation on most of America's religions, we made a special effort to gather data on those small groups which were doing the least about preserving their own history, either because they thought it unimportant or because they had no resources to establish permanent archives. ISAR set out to build a library with representative material from every religious group in the United States, later broadened to include all of North America. By the beginning of the 1980s we were somewhat confident that we had discerned a number of important trends in North American religion and had some grasp of the way into which the more nonconventional religions fit into that picture.

Along with collecting primary data from the newer religions, we have also tried to monitor the research and debates within the scholarly community. The cult wars have generated an avalanche of research on nonconventional religion. However, as the discussions developed, we have had to put aside many of the assumptions with which we began: 1) because they failed to be confirmed by the increasing amount of data, and 2) because we have recognized the role which the controversy has had in distorting our work. Let us briefly suggest one or two of the more important foundational hypotheses which were found to rest on shifting sand.

Firstly, we have overvalued the *role of the founder/leaders of new religions*. We assumed that the new religions were leader-oriented and that once the leader died, the groups would soon fade away. Although there were no examples of such over-reliance on a leader in the literature, it has been one of the hardest false assumptions to dislodge. However, in the wake of the deaths of a number of founder/leaders during the last fifteen years and the continuance of their movements, with hardly a skipped heartbeat, we can now safely discard that hypothesis.

New religions are certainly the extended shadow of their founders, but groups do not draw their life from the founders so much as participation in the founder's spiritual vision. No more impressive example has been given to us recently than that of Rajneesh. The Rajneesh movement, to all outward appearance, experienced three disasters one right after the other, any one of which could have mortally wounded it: the demise of its Oregon centre Rajneeshpuram, the deportation of its leader, and then the unexpected death of Rajneesh. However, careful monitoring of the movement revealed only a slight geographically-confined disruption. In the United States the movement quickly returned to its pre-Rajneeshpuram structure, decentralized into scattered ashrams, and carried on as it had done prior to the establishment of the community. Its international periodical never missed an issue, and its literature distribution never slowed. In Europe, where the movement was hardly affected by the existence of Rajneeshpuram, it simply continued as if nothing had happened.

Secondly, we need to balance the emphasis, inherent in our terminology, which accentuated the *discontinuity of current religious phenomena* over its continuity both with the past and with religion around the world. The current use of the term 'new religion', of course, is such a misnomer. In like measure, the popular meaning of the label 'cult', in the English-language press and anti-cult literature, has hypothesized a set of modern new technologies which are said to distinguish the new cults from the more traditional religions.

Possibly it is the bias of a historian who has been further influenced by readings in comparative religions, but it has become obvious that in spite of the recent origin of the disturbance of our consciousness by the new religious movements, their presence is simply the maturing of a long-term trend initiated in the last century, which in turn is deeply grounded in even very old tendencies in Western culture which have merely awaited the removal of the state's coercive restraints to emerge in force. We shall return to this point later. Coupled with this observation is our inability to locate any phenomenon in the so-called new religions which has not been present at the heart of the major religious traditions in force for centuries. The new gurus are doing nothing Hindu saints have not been teaching for millennia, the new occultists are doing nothing that cannot be fully documented in ancient Western literature. The techniques of the 'new religions' may occasionally be packaged a little more glamorously, but they are the same old conscious-altering techniques which religions have always advocated.

Thirdly, we need to re-evaluate our understanding of *the relation of religions to social unrest*. In order to explain the sudden appearance of so many 'new religions' in the San Francisco Bay area in the late 1960s, it was suggested that their emergence was due to the social disruptions of the counterculture of the 1960s. However, now that we stand at some distance from the 1960s, we can see the following: 1) For decades prior to that era the number of additions of new members to the community of religious groups has been steadily growing; 2) that the process of growth has continued unabated to the present moment; and 3) that there is every reason to believe that the rate of growth will not only continue through to the end of the century but accelerate.

In the 1970s there was little data upon which to tie together new religions and social unrest apart from the happenstance of the intense reality of the Berkeley scene. The immediate reference point seems to have been the reported burst of new religions in Japan following the disruptions of World War II. We now know that the image of a sudden explosion of new religions in Japan in the late 1940s is an over simplification, to say the least. The religions which suddenly became visible to observers in the 1950s had been founded one by one through the decades of the nineteenth and twentieth century, some as schisms of the older religions, some as attempts to synthesize the older traditions, and some as imports from the West. However, during the twentieth century, these new religions were systematically suppressed. Then in 1945 under the pressure of the United States occupation, the Japanese government abandoned the legal sanctions against the new religions. They suddenly emerged into view, although they had been there for decades.

A similar situation developed in Berkeley in the late-1960s when a group of scholars suddenly saw a number of unfamiliar religions operating within the counterculture. The vast majority of these 'new religions' had been around for over a decade, and many for a number of decades (Gurdjieff, Meher Baba, the Sufi Order). There were some genuinly new ones, almost all of which were from Asia. Missed was the observation that in 1965 the United States, just as Japan had twenty years earlier,passed through a significant legal change. In 1965 the remnants of the Oriental Exclusion Act were tossed in the rubbish bin and for the first time since 1924 massive immigration of Asians was encouraged. From this beginning in 1965, the growth rate of new religious organizations only slightly accelerated, while the exotic component accelerated at an extraordinary pace.

Not a small part of the disenchantment with the social unrest theories is the largely unspoken but very real assumption upon which such theories rest, namely that religious phenomena is epiphenomenal — that it is primarily a product and effect, rather than a change agent and a cause, whose action upon the culture needs to be understood every bit as much as any reciprocal altering of religion by the environment. This unspoken assumption, of course, has a direct bearing upon our perception of new religions, especially if we could reduce them merely to a response to the culture.

The survival of these three assumptions, and others which we could enumerate, was based in large part on the over-concentration of our attention and studies on a few atypical groups, rather than broadly gathering data from the several hundred nonconventional religions available to us. Well over half the studies of new religions we undertook in the last 15 years concerned the Unification Church, and the next largest pile is from the International Society for Krishna Consciousness and its offshoots. While knowledge of these two groups is important, both are so atypical that our data on them yields very little information about religious trends in general. They have proven very poor weather vanes by which to discern the future directions in which the nonconventional religious winds will be blowing.

Europe and the Development of American Religion

Thus by the time we began the European work, we had cast aside the assumptions just enumerated. These had not been the hardest ones to put aside, for over the years the data we had accumulated had also contradicted some of the basic assumptions in the standard writing of American religious history. Also, I must admit a certain reluctance in accepting the trends that the data revealed. Having been trained as a church historian, I found it difficult to handle the information which ran counter to images of American religious life which had been hammered into me as an eager young graduate student. I had been taught of the flourishing era of the colonial church and its fall into spiritual coldness, though not so dead as to miss participation in the American Revolution and the development of its freedom ideals. The nineteenth century was an era of church growth as the population expanded, the older churches received new members, and new churches (Methodists and Baptists) came on the scene. There were even some Roman Catholics on the periphery.

The golden era for Protestantism lasted through World War II, but problems were developing. Secularism was arising and sapping the church's strength, challenging it for the allegiance of the American people. Roman Catholicism had come out of World War II fighting for recognition. Protestant church growth slowed to a trickle and then began to turn downward. Massive programmes were demanded to meet the contemporary needs of people and recapture the church's relevance. As those programmes failed, the mainline Protestant churches experienced a downward membership trend which had left them somewhat bewildered about what was happening to them and what could be done about it.

Meanwhile, a much different picture was being outlined as we synthesized data from our periodic surveys of American religious groups with other data such as that compiled by Gaustad in his Religious Atlas, the old religious censuses, the annual *Yearbook of American Churches*, and recent public surveys, not least of which was the one still in process of publication by colleagues Phillip Hammond and Clark Wade Roof.

The emerging picture revealed a colonial American population largely detached from organized religion. While there were religious enclaves in New England, Philadelphia, and other centres settled by religious dissidents, the majority of the population derived from those elements of European society with the least investment in European cultural norms, including its traditional religious life. They were the people with the least to lose by leaving, and they manifested their alienation in part, both by their non-support of religious structures and the ready tolerance of anti-clericalism in their leaders.

Such anti-clericalism peaked in North America in the late-eighteenth century, and undergirded the placing of the First Amendment in the United States Constitution. Once the Revolutionary dust settled, church leaders (outside of New England) realized the disaster that had befallen them. Their work (and leadership) had been decimated by the war itself; their income had been cut off; and an unchurched western land was beginning to fill up with people in need of religious guidance. It is to the churches' credit that they seized the moment and began an unprecedented period of growth. For over 150 years religious affiliation in this country rose steadily as membership went from something less than 20% to approximately 70%. Leading that growth was Roman Catholicism, which in 1844 became the largest church body in America and which never looked back.

Throughout the nineteenth century there was a steady growth in religious or organizational membership, the rate of which stayed well ahead of population growth throughout the nineteenth century. Then between 1900 and 1980, as the population grew 3½ times, religious affiliation grew 7 times. However, the good news for religions was tempered by the recognition of a second trend.

The percentage of the population adhering to the older Protestant churches, the so-called 'mainline', fell steadily. While still possessing a large membership and having accumulated considerable wealth in real estate and stock port folios, they failed to move with the development of society, and after World War II not only failed to grow, but actually began to lose members. Thus, while society was becoming more and more 'religious', the older liberal Protestant churches were experiencing a down-swing that as yet shows no sign of being reversed.

New Religions

But how do the 'new religions' fit into the scenario? Their story began in the nineteenth century with the emergence of some genuine new religious movements in America. We know their names — Spiritualism, Mormonism, Adventism (including the Jehovah's Witnesses), Theosophy, Christian Science, New Thought. These were America's contribution to world religion. By 1893 these were all firmly established in North America and were spreading across the Atlantic to Europe. As each emerged, it attracted the attention of the older religious community and was denounced.

Then in the 1880s, a new element was added — Eastern religions. Both Buddhism and Hinduism, which have been present peripherally for decades, developed a noticeable following outside of the Asian-American community, and the 1890s saw the formation of the original Hindu and Buddhist organizations. Islam followed a decade later.

Once introduced, Eastern and Islamic religion flourished for a generation. It grew by the same processes as the older groups, the immigration of the faithful from the old country and the gaining of converts in the new. But the steady growth of Eastern religions was abruptly halted in 1924 with the passing of the comprehensive immigration bill that cut off further Asian entry into the country. It was the reversal of the policy of the 1924 immigration bill, and the immediate response of Asians wishing to move into the United States after 1965, which allowed the sudden emergence of a new wave of Asian religion in America (and Canada).

Thus, growing up beside the Christian churches were expansive nonconventional religious communities. Throughout the nineteenth and twentieth century there has been a steady growth of nonconventional religion in America in almost every area of the country, but especially in the Northern urban centres and more recently along the West coast. California, the only state with three major urban complexes has become a popular home for new religions. The old nineteenth-century groups, with a few notable exceptions (for example, the Church of Christ, Scientist), have shown a steady growth and a few, such as the Mormons and Jehovah's Witnesses, have shown a spectacular international spread. While the older groups continued to spread, since 1965 they have been joined by Buddhists, Hindus, Sikhs, and Muslims in North America. Overall the rise of new religions has been unaffected by the presence of the anti-cult movement, though individual groups have had to adjust their priorities in order to counter the attacks against them. The future appears bright. The former President, George Bush, signed a new immigration law which raised the quota on Asian immigration by 60%. I suggest that the number of new Asian religions and their adherents will take another steep upward swing through the 1990s.

But what about Europe?

It was during the process of creating the picture of American religious growth that the issue of Europe was injected. Rodney Stark authored several papers in which he argued, on grounds which were as foreign to me as was contemporary European religion at the time, that if his reflections about the nature of religion and secularization were true, then Europe should also be experiencing a high level presence of new religions, as high — if not higher — than the United States. His conclusions sounded perfectly reasonable to me, not because I fully understood and agreed with his argument, but for two other reasons. Firstly, from going over the accounts of Asian religions which had come to the United States, it became obvious that the Asian religions had launched their migration into Europe during the twenty years immediately after World War II and only arrived in the United States after 1965. Because they came into Europe more quietly, they were not noticed until the 1970s, after the alarm was sounded at Berkeley. Also throughout the twentieth century, America had received a constant stream of new occult religions which had been founded in Europe.

Secondly, I had reasoned, if secularism had progressed in Europe to the extent observers confirmed it had, then the drop in allegiance to the older churches would have created a religious vacuum which the new religions could help fill. However, neither of us had the data to work from. Rod urged me to collect it. I refused knowing that gathering the necessary information could not be done without field work, and that I had a big enough job just keeping up with the dynamic North American scene.

Then two years ago I was approached by Robert Moore, the new director of the Institute of World Spirituality. He asked me to conduct that institute's first research programme: to prepare an international directory of the world's religions. After some initial resistance I agreed, and our staff in Santa Barbara began work on Canada, the United Kingdom and Ireland, and continental Europe. The first volumes of the *Religious Directory International* are now published. The work of preparing these directories not only took a significant amount of staff time by two people but also involved four data gathering trips to Europe by myself and one by Isotta Poggi, my assistant, who also served as the associate editor of the volume.

Because of the nature of the original request and the stipulation of the grant which initiated the research, we did not limit our search to non-conventional religions. Rather, we were to survey the whole religious community, assess its divisions, and determine the extent of its pluralism. At the point we began, we knew that Europe had developed a level of pluralism, but had no idea of its extent. In our initial assembling of data on the Christian churches, we discovered, that like the United States, European Christianity is now fractured into literally hundreds of denominations, far more than Barrett reported in his *World Christian Encyclopedia* in 1982. That was somewhat to be expected.

Far more interesting, however, were the hundreds of esoteric Christian and non-Christian religions which we were able to locate with little trouble. Very quickly we discovered that the European religious community had, in a manner similar to its American counterparts, developed a series of religious networks. For our purposes, the primary network consisted of the many metaphysical bookstores which cater to the occult, New Age, and Eastern spiritualities. The bookstores form what amounts to a meta-network for these alternative spiritualities. The literature available at these stores provided a relatively easy entry into the world of alternatives to the older Churches. We found ourselves on familiar ground, since we located virtually the same alternatives that were available in the United States.

The directories we compiled gave us a bird's eye view of the vast number of new religions in Europe. They confirmed that, country by country, Europe has welcomed far more new religions (per million persons in the population) than the United States. In countries such as the United Kingdom, Switzerland and Holland, the figures are very high, but even in Italy and Spain, they are noticeable. They are lowest in countries such as Greece, Bulgaria, and Finland. We are aware, that in every case, the number of new religions is consistently under-reported.

In examining the networks, we also noted the existence of another similarity between Europe and America. Namely, apart from the bookstores, no network of new religions per se exists, and only very limited ongoing contact exists directly between them. On the other hand, new religious groups which follow a Buddhist practice similar to that practiced by ethnic Buddhist groups share a common network. There is also a network of Hindu groups, which includes both the newer organizations such as the Hare Krishna, and the ethnic Hindu groups. There is a network of Wiccan groups and likewise of theosophical-New Age groups. The nature of the social configurations indicate that the new religious movements are best defined as variations of the older religious traditions and are so accepted and acknowledged by the leaders of the older religious communities. One misunderstands the new religions apart from some comprehension of their role as perpetuators of an old tradition.

From our directories, and what is known generally about the history of alternative religions in Europe, we can put together in broad terms a picture of their development and project a possible future. The Napoleonic era shook the European religious establishment as it introduced significant new privileges for religious minorities, and from that time we can notice a decrease of public support for the older state churches across the continent. As the laws limiting religious freedom changed, new religions appeared. Some came from North America — Spiritualism and Theosophy most notably. However, one also notices the development of new European movements generated without any particular reference to North America. The modern occult revival, for example, was not created by Americans but by the likes of Austrian Franz Mesmer, Swedish Emanuel Swedenborg,

Frenchmen Louis Claude de Saint Martin, Eliphas Levi, and Papus, plus, of course, Britain's own Aleister Crowley. In addition, between 1800 and 1945, across Europe, in every country without significant legal restraints, new innovative religions emerged along the same spectrum as were appearing in North America. A list of the more important would include the Panacea Society (England), Anthroposophy (Germany), the Martinus Institute of Spiritual Science (Denmark), the Church of the Reign of God (Switzerland), the Lectorium Rosicrucianum (the Netherlands), the Ordo Templi Orientis (Germany), and the Grail Movement (Austria).

As in the United States, Eastern religion filtered into Europe in the late nineteenth century, and experienced a slow growth through the twentieth century. Periodic wars stifled it, but there was no abrupt stopping and starting again as in the United States, though we can now see that following World War II and the declaration of Indian independence, the number of Eastern teachers migrating to Europe and the number of Europeans going to the East on spiritual quests increased abruptly. Over the last 45 years a steady but growing stream of Eastern teachers and new Western esoteric teachers have opened their centres in Europe.

We must note, however, that once observers noticed the new religions in the 1970s, a quite mistaken notion entered into the literature and became somewhat of a truism. Not having experienced a sudden appearance of new religions, as was believed to have occurred in Berkeley, and as European observers discovered more and more groups through the 1970s, many came to believe that the new religions of Europe resulted from the migration eastward across the Atlantic of a phenomenon already well-developed in California. I first encountered the idea in an article concerning Bhagwan Rajneesh which opened with the authoritative pronouncement:

The religious groups with a Hindu or Buddist background that reached Europe in the 1960s and 1970s came *without exception* by way of the United States and penetrated the Old World in an 'Americanised' form.[1]

The authors then continued their discussion of Rajneesh completely oblivious to the fact that Rajneesh's movement had spread across Europe for a decade (as had most of the other Asian religions) before making its initial appearance in the United States. More recently, similar observations have been made about the

New Age Movement, a movement which originated in Europe among a network of British theosophical groups and was exported from there both to the United States and to continental Europe (where it today enjoys an even greater public appeal for its ideas than it does in North America).

Quite apart from the mistake inherent in the Rajneesh article quoted above, there is a second, more legitimate reason for the development of a belief that Europe's new religions' scene has derived from the United States. Beginning in 1945 a major religious movement was launched in Europe from America: the missionizing of Europe by free church evangelical Christians. Throughout the entire twentieth century North Americans heard stories about the secularization of Europe. Evangelical Christians took those stories, constantly confirmed in the jeremiads of European church leaders, very seriously. They assumed as true the words of World Council of Churches president and Lutheran Bishop Hans Lilje, 'The era when Europe was a Christian continent lies behind us.'[2] And, if it is true that Europe is no longer Christian, then it is a fitting target for missionary activity.

Thus immediately after World War II, American missionary agencies began to target Europe. From bases in such places as London, Monte Carlo and Luxembourg, they fanned out across Europe, and as restrictive laws fell, entered country after country. Today, more than 200 missionary agencies operate in Europe from home offices in North America. Among the more prominent of the missionary organization are Youth for Christ International, Young Life, and Youth with a Mission, not to mention the many groups which use college students on short term missions in the summer. It is easy to confuse the far more successful activity of the evangelical Christian groups which have founded thousands of congregations in Europe since 1945 with the metaphysical, occult and Asian new religious groups. And certainly, the secular anti-cult movement frequently lumps the two groups together.

Conclusion

We can very quickly summarize three primary conclusions about Europe's new religious movements. Firstly, overall European receptivitiy of new religions is as high if not higher than in the United States. Somewhere approaching one third of all the religious bodies currently operating in Europe are nonconventional religions — metaphysical, esoteric, Asian. The only places where they have not appeared or that their development lags behind are in those countries which still use the state to prohibit religious freedom. That being the case, the opening up of Eastern Europe has led to a remarkable spread of the new religions into places such as Romania, Hungary, and Albania.

Secondly, a number of the Asian groups are primarily ethnic in origin, and are doing little to evangelize among non-Asians. However, as a whole, the 'new religions' which are actively proselytizing primarily young adult Europeans, are not new religions as such but are branches of older Asian religions which have developed an evangelistic zeal. They continue to look to the older and larger Buddhist, Hindu, Sikh, Jain, and Sant Mat ethnic communities as their religious base and are thus best understood as part of the overall diffusion of Eastern religion around the world.

Thirdly, while a large number of new religions exist in both the United States and Europe, they are still a long way from challenging the hegemony of Christianity as the dominant preferred religion. Compared to the many Christian church groups, the new religious movements are small and still politically weak. Only by aligning themselves with the larger ethnic communities can they begin to participate in the secular community as actors and then only as a minority group.

The significance of this first generation of the new religions is not in their numbers, they are still relatively small in the West, but rather lies in their establishment of a stable beachhead in the culture from which they can move into more and more communities and penetrate different social groups. Their future growth now depends upon their ability to adjust to European society and the level of the social reaction to their development.

Notes

1. Emphasis added. Reinhart Hummel and Bert Hardin, 'Asiatic Religions in Europe', in *New Religious Movements*, John Coleman and Gregory Baum (eds.), Edinburgh: T.T. Clark, 1983, 23.
2. Quoted in J. Herbert Kane, *A Global View of Christian Missions*, Grand Rapids, Mich. Baker Book House, 1971, 535.

CHAPTER 3

The Catholic Church and New Religions

Teresa Gonçalves

Introduction

'The Church, called to witness to Christ in Europe on the eve of the third millenium, has to find concrete ways of carrying this good news to those in the Old Continent who seem to have lost it'... So said John Paul II in October 1989 to the European Bishops at their VII Symposium, urging them on to the 'demanding' but 'inspiring' task of helping contemporary man to understand life and death. He added: 'Christianity, which once offered Europe in its formative stage the ideal values on which to build its unity, today has the task of revitalizing from within a civilization that shows preoccupying signs of decrepitude.'[1]

On that occasion the Holy Father referred to the way which in Europe today the reality of birth and death was being lived. European culture is in the midst of a crisis in the understanding of existence, and an ignorance of Jesus Christ as the One who revealed it, being Himself the Way, the Truth and the Life. This crisis could be connected with the spread in the West during the last decades of a large number of New Religious Movements (NRMs), deriving mainly from outside sources, but today firmly rooted among us.

Causes of the Emergence and Spreading of NRMs

What are the causes of this appearance of NRMs, in their multiple worldwide forms? The document of the Holy See on this subject, published in 1986, principally analyses the internal causes inherent in our society, that is, the needs and aspirations to which the sects appear to give an answer.[2] In other words, it indicates why today there is a fertile ground for NRMs. The document describes these aspirations as 'so many expressions of the human search for wholeness and harmony, participation and realization on all levels of human existence and experience as so many attempts to meet the human quest for truth and meaning of existence.'

This point of view is universally applicable because it is bound up with the general idea of 'religion', and implies a positive evaluation of the religious causes at the root of the problem. From this angle it is clear that the Church feels challenged as it realizes that many are not touched by the authentic Gospel message, which could fill the void they experience.

In order to interpret correctly the phenomenon of the expansion of NRMs and draw balanced pastoral conclusions, it is vital to grasp 'external' causes as well, such as increased human mobility, a growing cultural interdependence in our world as well as the power of social communications and international strategies for spreading these movements.

In this matter valuable elements can be found in the Acts of the Consultation organized in 1986 at Amsterdam by the World Lutheran Federation and the World Council of Churches.[3] They highlight among other things the American origin of a great number of NRMs present today in Europe and Third World countries, including those with oriental roots that were transplanted into the USA. However diversified, these religious messages spread under their American cultural forms which have deeply impressed young people from the 1960s onwards.

More light will be thrown on this problem through the research on NRMs being undertaken on a worldwide scale by the International Federation of Catholic Universities in response to an invitation from the Holy See.

The Church's Concern and Reflection

The Catholic Church has looked into the problem of NRMs from various angles and from different contexts. For instance, when she speaks of a 'New Evangelization', or in preparing documents for the Synod on priestly formation, or for the African synod, or when analysing the situation of each local Church during the Ad Limina visits. Even when NRMs are not explicitly referred to, we shed light on these realities in many pontifical documents and at meetings promoted by the Holy See.

The reflection of the Catholic Church on ecclesial movements — which have developed over the last 30-40 years — can offer interesting suggestions for our theme. The Synod on the Laity in 1987 paid great attention to these ecclesial movements. In the post-synodal exhortation they were spoken of as one of the many signs of the Spirit at work as it 'continues to renew the youth of the Church and to inspire new aspirations towards holiness and solidarity'.[4] Would it be too much to conclude that the same Spirit, questioning the Church with the growing number of religious alternatives, is stirring up answers within the Church in the form of new-style communities and spiritual experiences? This would explain in a positive sense some analogies which can be found between NRMs and ecclesial movements. However, it should be stressed that the essential mark of these ecclesial movements is communion of faith and charity, which the Pontifical Exhortation develops by setting out five criteria of ecclesiality: 1) primacy given to the call to holiness for every Christian; 2) responsibility to confess the Catholic faith; 3) testimony to a strong and convinced filial communion with the pastors of the Church; 4) collaboration with other apostolic groups, and, finally, 5) commitment to be present in human society.

Confidence in the specific contribution of the ecclesial movements caused the Pontifical Council for the Pastoral Care of Migrants and Itinerant People to invite representatives of three movements to their plenary assembly in October 1989 on the theme 'Spread of the sects: Dimension and causes in the context of human mobility'. Attention was brought to bear on the vulnerability of migrants and refugees, uprooted from their cultural, social and family milieu, and often shaken in their religious convictions. The testimony of lay representatives highlighted experiences of faith open to all layfolk, awareness and concern for people living on the outskirts of the big cities, and a dialogical attitude and collaboration with everyone, including foreigners and persons with other ideologies. On the whole these witnesses evidenced an open Church that is close to every man and woman.

Certain tendencies of the 'new religiosity' in the West show a concern that is addressed in the Letter of the Congregation for the Doctrine of the Faith: 'Some aspects of Christian Meditation'.[5] The Letter does not question authentic interreligious dialogue, even in its dimension of spiritual exchange, but calls attention to the danger of syncretism, when superficial and scantily formed Christians seek spiritual experiences through methods used by these religions. The danger would be, says the Letter, that the one praying would be imprisoned 'in a spiritual privatism which is incapable of a free openness to the transcendental God' (n. 3). When we read this document we feel challenged as believers who have experienced, as the Letter says, the joy of the 'flight from 'self' to the 'you' of God' (n. 1), and so feel the responsibility for sharing this great gift with others.

The reflection of the Church is also stimulated by historical circumstances of exceptional importance, such as the fall of Communism and the opening of the frontiers between East and West Europe. In this context we could provide ample evidence of the religious spirit which official atheism was unable to uproot and of the spiritual demands of the peoples of the East. Their manifest desire for more religious information, shown on so many occasions, opens up fresh opportunities in the field of social communications, a theme discussed in Fatima at the meeting of the European Bishops in charge of mass media, 22-23 March 1990. At the same time it has become evident that Western Europe is a channel to the Eastern countries not only for Christianity, but for a thousand new religious movements.

Other challenges coming from non-European continents rise to the surface as two great events draw near: the African Synod and the Fifth Centenary of the Evangelization of America. These are occasions for the Church to reflect on the quality of its missionary activity, its capacity for inculturation, and the very concept of mission in a world where more and more importance is given to religious pluralism.

Interreligious dialogue is looked upon more and more as an essential element of the mission of the Church, as was noted in a document published in 1984 by the Pontifical Council for Interreligious Dialogue.[6] As a symbol of the new attitude everyone remembers the interreligious Day of Prayer for Peace in Assisi in 1986. That day was an affirmation of the basic unity of God's plan in creation and redemption that embraces the universe and all peoples. Two months later the Pope, addressing the Roman Curia, called this unity more fundamental and decisive than all religious differences and divergences, and should be overcome in the progress towards carrying out the great design of unity in creation itself.[7]

Can we fit the NRMs into this perspective? For the moment the Catholic Church has taken no official position on dialogue with

NRMs, and perhaps there cannot be an all-inclusive position; each NRM has to be taken on its own and the way each case develops will be observed. But the Holy Father's remarks on 'differences' to be overcome may enlighten us:

There are undeniably differences that reflect the genius and the spiritual 'riches' which God has given to the people (...) I am not referring to these divergences; I intend here to speak of the differences in which are revealed the limits, the evolution and the fall of the human spirit which is undermined by the spirit of evil in history.[8]

This explanation brings us to the duty of fulfilling the difficult task of discerning the authentic values in every expression of religiosity whether it be individual or collective.

On the other hand there are no limits to dialogue on a personal level, as there is no limit to the love of God for all men and women. As Paul VI says in 'Ecclesiam Suam':[9]

Wherever men are trying to understand themselves and the world, we can communicate with them(...) If there exists in men a soul naturally Christian, we desire to show it our respect and to enter into conversation with it.

These words have to do with the attitude of dialogue towards all men and therefore can be applied to all members of NRMs, whatever their origins. 'In the dialogue', Paul VI goes on,

one discovers how different are the ways which lead to the light of faith, and how it is possible to make them complementary by forcing our reasoning process out of the worn paths and by obliging it to deepen its research to find fresh expressions.

Notes

1. John Paul II, 'Address to the participants in the VII European Bishop's Symposium', in *L'Osservatore Romano*, October 18, 1989.
2. Secretariat for Promoting Christian Unity, Sec. for Non-Christians, Sec. for Non-Believers, Pontifical Council for Culture, *Sects or New Religious Movements: pastoral challenge*, May 3,1986. We can find other pastoral approaches in an anthology published after the Lugano conference by the Working Group on New Religious Movements, Vatican City. The English edition has been published in 1995 by the

United States Catholic Conference, Washington, under the title *Sects and New Religious Movements*. An Anthology of Texts from the Catholic Church, 1986-1994.

3. Cf. *New Religious Movements and the Churches*, Report and papers of a consultation sponsored by the Lutheran World Federation and the World Council of Churches, Geneva: WCC Publications, 1987.

4. John Paul II, *Post-Synodal Apostolic Exhortation 'Christifideles Laici' on the Vocation and Mission of the Lay Faithful in the Church and in the World*, December 30, 1988, Typis Polyglottis Vaticanis.

5. Congregation for the Doctrine of Faith, *Letter to the Bishop of the Catholic Church on some Aspects of Christian Meditation*, October 15, 1989, Typis Polyglottis Vaticanis.

6. Secretariatus for Non Christians, *The attitude of the Church towards the followers of other religions. Reflections and orientations on Dialogue and Mission*, Pentecost 1984, Typis Polyglottis Vaticanis.

7. John Paul II, 'Address to the Cardinals and to the Roman Curia', in *L'Osservatore Romano*, December 22, 1986.

8. *Ibid*.

9. Paul VI, *Ecclesiam Suam. Encyclical Letter to the Episcopate, to the clergy, to the faithful, to all men of good will*, August 6, 1964, Typis Polyglottis Vaticanis.

CHAPTER 4

Confronting the New Religious Movements in Greece

Antonios Alevisopoulos

The appearance in Greece of the New Religious Movements is relatively new. Movements of past centuries that arrived in our country are mainly Anthroposophy, Freemasonry and Christian Science. However, under the movements of neo-paganism and neo-idolatry, there has appeared in recent times a tendency towards a revival of the ancient Greek gods and their worship.

During the decade of the 1970s many guru organizations arrived in Greece, in particular organizations of Maharishi Mahesh Yogi, Maharaj Ji and Swami Prabhupada (Hare Krishna). In the meantime, the various yoga organizations that are led by a guru, multiplied, and the Greek scene is quite similar to the other European Community countries. Various psycho-cults such as Scientology, political religions and new heresies such as Ananda Marga, New Acropolis and the Moon movement, are active. Also active are various neo-gnostic movements like the branches of the heritage of Samael Aum Veor. There is also a great variety of occult organizations (spiritualistic, mediumistic, neo-satanists etc.). There are also many Buddhist and Islamic heresies, such as Ba'hai, Soufis, and others. Unfortunately, Greece does not have any kind of research centre pertaining to those matters. For this reason we won't guess by mentioning any statistics.

Along with all these various groups there are also other occult beliefs such as astrology, the belief in Karma and reincarnation and many other occult beliefs taken from the occult and magic areas, that threaten to corrode the spiritual and cultural ways of our country, because all of them keep gaining ground.

The Orthodox Church confronts these phenomena mainly by the spiritual life within the Church. That is, not only with catechism and sermons, but with the participation in the sacramental life of the church and in particular with the participation in the Holy Confession. The richness of the Orthodox worship and the holy symbols touch on not only a person's rationality, but his whole life. Inside the Church, the Orthodox believer hears, sees, smells, touches and thinks. In other words, he is totally involved and he is invited to take part in the mystery of his faith, the liturgy and prayer.

Consequently, the Orthodox believer, depending on the degree that he actually lives the Church's life and how conscious he is of his faith, does not have any voids and he is protected from the adventure of a false quest.

Beyond all the things mentioned above, the Church of Greece during the decade of the 1970s became very active on this matter. It created a special synodal commission under the direction of Protopresbyter Antonios Alevisopoulos, Dr Theol., Dr Phil., while the Athens Archdiocese created the Office of Orthodox Apologetics and the Orthodox Advanced Centre on Research and Dialogue (OACRD). These two offices are under the direction of the same person. Together with these two, Father Alevisopoulos took the initiative and created the Pan-Hellenic Parents' Association for the Protection of the Greek-Orthodox Culture, the Family and the Individual (PPU) which is being used as an instrument to prepare various programmes, mainly informative, educational, publishing books of local, national, inter-orthodox and international level.

These activities cover the following areas:

a) *Research*

A special work team was created mainly from young people and ex-members, who study in depth the organizations at an international level and publish suitable books. These books pertain to the setting of the boundaries of the Orthodox faith in relation to the challenge of the new movements. These books are:
Aid to the Understanding of Orthodoxy
The Orthodox Church. Faith — Worship — Life
Our Orthodoxy

Neo-Protestants, Fundamentalist Sects:
Handbook of Heretical and para-Christian sects

Non-Christian religions and para-Christian groups:
Occultism, Guruism, New Age

Self-knowledge, Self-evolution, Salvation
Reincarnation or resurrection? The Orthodox View of the Evil
Spiritual Rape. New cults, a Real Threat
Meditation or Prayer?
Documents Regarding Sects and Cults

Jehovah's Witnesses. This is the three volume work *Watch Tower Cult, Older and newer history*, based on known and unknown sources, and the *Dictatorship of Brooklyn*

b) *Educational Programmes*

We have a four-month specialized educational seminar for the work team. The climax of this seminar is a yearly ten-day seminar of faith with cenobitic life. In these seminars, the problems of the present situation are discussed from every angle, and new lectures are prepared for further educational programmes. On a national and inter-orthodox level we have annual five-day consultations. Also we have a programme called 'The Orthodox Theological Seminar'.

These programmes are under the auspices of the Archbishop of Athens and all of Greece, Mr Seraphim, and are being organized by PPU and OACRD. PPU has already successfully organized three specialized international conferences. The delegates of all the Orthodox Churches are members of PPU and OACRD. During the Third International Conference of Pendeli (November 1993), the Inter-Orthodox Association of Parents was created to function as a partner in the international cooperation and also in the educational area.

Young persons that have been associated with the cults or are having problems due to these cults can contact us during the four-month seminar of Orthodox Faith. The lecturers of this seminar are from the wide Orthodox area. This work is followed by another seminar of edification in Orthodoxy and re-integration that functions every Sunday all year round.

c) *Advisory Service*

This functions every Sunday morning with the cooperation of volunteer help, all of them graduates of our seminars. At the Advisory Service Social Workers and ex-victims also work.

d) *Secretariat*

Until October 1993 this service was offered completely by volunteers. Volunteers gave all the lectures both in the Orthodox and international areas. The hospitality was offered by the Holy Synod and by various bishopies. However, the growth of the work, particularly at the inter-orthodox level, obliged us to organize an economic campaign. In order to create a permanent basis for the international and inter-orthodox secretariat, we are now trying to find sponsors. A permanent secretariat is of utmost importance for our work so that we may be able to realize the resolutions that were taken and included in the Proclamation of Pendeli, regarding international cooperation.

The Holy Synod of the Greek Church has been very active with this subject. Beyond these initiatives they have issued from time to time special circulars and instructions concerning specific groups in connection with this matter, such as The Children of God, Hare Krishna, Moon movement, Scientology, Witchcraft, Satanism, among others.

The Holy Synod recently declared as deviant and incompatible with the Orthodox Religion's 129 groups, which are incorporated in a special catalogue issued by the Orthodox Conference authorised to deal with matters concerning heresies and parareligious groups (May 1993).

The Greek State and particularly the Greek Parliament have neither dealt officially with this matter, nor have they taken any official stand during the 1984 Euro-parliament ballot or the relevant directives of the 1992 European Council, in spite of the fact that since February 1993 both the Archbishop and the appropriate Department of Information, Dialogue and Civilization underlined the importance of cooperation with the State in the form of special publications.

At the beginning of 1994, as a result of the two ritualistic murders performed by satanists which completely energised the public opinion, a cooperation commenced between the Church (OACRD), responsible ministries, and the local authorities through the new body of PPU, having its headquarters in the suburb of Agia Paraskevi, but without any relation to the economic support of the programme. According to the directives of the Ministry of Education, persons and officers from the Tutorial sector are participating in these seminars.

We are rather optimistic that the new programmes will not only be continued but enlarged as well. This however,is principally dependent on the economic infrastructure and support. The annual budget necessary is 14 million drachmas (US$54,000 approximately).

In connection with the above, it should be underlined that there is a prime piece of land available which can be used to erect a special research centre for the whole of Orthodoxy, provided the necessary financial resources can be found.

The last attack, mainly on the part of Scientology, proved how necessary the international cooperation is, and how important it is to stand by each other. We are grateful for all the worldwide parents' initiatives who are sending us their printed material containing indispensable information, all of which is valuable for all the Eastern European countries. The Inter-Orthodox Association and the PPU are the only centres of this information in this geographical area.

CHAPTER 5

New Religious Movements in Italy

Massimo Introvigne & Gianni Ambrosio

Introduction: What is a 'new' religious movement?

In March 1990 CESNUR, the Centre for Studies on New Religions, asked a company specializing in market surveys to perform a sample survey in downtown Turin among the general public about their perception of 'new religious movements'. The results (see appendix 1) show that neither 'new religious movements' nor 'new religions' are really part of the general language in Italy. 'Culto' (cult) normally means a devotion *within* the Catholic Church (e.g. 'cult of the Sacred Heart'), although scholars sometimes use 'nuovi culti' (new cults) to designate all or some new religious movements. Scholars may limit their use of 'setta' (sect) to groups of Christian origins like the Jehovah's Witnesses or the Mormons. Our survey, however, confirms that a large majority of the Italian public use the word 'sect' to designate both historical Christian sects like the Mormons and new religious movements like the Unification Church or the Church of Scientology. Additionally, the survey shows that 40% of the Italian public normally understand the word 'sect' and relate it to some sort of social problem, 25% understand the term 'new religions', while — as mentioned earlier — very few people understand what a question concerning 'new religious movements' or 'new cults' means. 'Sects' are perceived by 80% of the Italian public as something negative and/or dangerous (hence the scholarly preference for some other word). When requested to mention a typical 'sect', 80% of the public mentioned the Jehovah's Witnesses, with a 13.3% reference to the Mormons and very few and vague references to other groups (including Scientology).

Indeed, a specific feature of Italy seems to be the almost immediate link in the popular perception between the 'problem of the sects' and Jehovah's Witnesses. Some years ago, a famous deprogrammer invited to Italy by a small anti-cult group, was rather astonished to discover that a large majority of the questions concerned Jehovah's Witnesses. Although the founder of that group was originally concerned with Scientology, the deprogrammer soon discovered (and investigations we performed have confirmed) that most people who contacted this group (called ARIS) were in fact only concerned with Jehovah's Witnesses and knew almost nothing — and cared less — about Scientology, the Hare Krishnas or the Moonies. Having emphasized the role of Jehovah's Witnesses in the public perception of the 'sects' (well grounded in the figures: there are in Italy more than 400,000 Jehovah's Witnesses — including the non-active — and less than 300 full-time Moonies), we should perhaps remark, once again, on the difficulties inherent in a general definition of 'sects', 'cults' and 'new religions' independent from a specific country or time.

The Italian background

It is impossible to understand the rise of Christian 'sects' and of new religious movements in Italy without at least a quick look at the general religious background in the last century. We would offer a very general summary of some themes discussed by historians and sociologists with reference to the Monarchy of Italy (1861-1946) and to the subsequent republic (1946). For a number of reasons, we do not believe that the Fascist period (1922-1945) altered the religious situation of the Monarchy substantially. It is true that minority religions were discriminated against by the Fascist government, but discrimination began in the nineteenth century and lasted into the 1950s and 1960s.

The Monarchy (1870-1946)

The Monarchy of Italy was basically the historical result of the project of a small minority (the ruling class) who built the modern Italian state and ruled it with very little participation from a large majority of the Italians (the people). One should remember that after the conquest of Rome (1870) the Catholic Church ordered the Catholics, under penalty of excommunication, not to vote nor to run in Italian elections. The vast majority of Catholics accepted this prohibition and virtually excluded themselves from political and administrative power (with some exceptions allowed by the Church) until World War II. Although Roman Catholicism was theoretically the religion of the Italian State, the country was ruled — economically as well as politically — by non-Catholics and each new King was routinely excommunicated by the Popes until 1929 (the year of the treaty between the Vatican and Mussolini). On this background:

a) *The ruling class* had few Catholics within its ranks (and these Catholics tended to absorb the values of the ruling class rather than vice versa) and was often very hostile to the Catholic Church (in the years 1861-1864 nine Italian Cardinals found themselves in Italian jails under various pretexts, which is more than Stalin himself managed to put in jail at any time). This class was not without religious interests; it had a great respect for Protestantism, even if devoted more to a mythical image of a liberal Christianity far from Catholic reactionary politics than to the real Protantism. Many authors of the ruling class liked to relate the economic and political growth of countries like England to Protestantism, and the delays of the Italian economy and institutions (well before Max Weber) to the lack of a Protestant Reformation in the country; some went so far as to promote and support, in Italy, Protestant missions from the United Kingdom, and later the United States. But, while willing to contribute some money to these missions, few members of the ruling class were actually prepared to convert to Protestantism.

They had a routine connection with Freemasonry whose larger branch in Italy severed ties in the nineteenth century with the Grand Lodge of England (as happened in France) for its extreme anti-Catholic and sometimes atheistic bias. A wing of the Freemasons was however very interested in occultism and in several varieties of esoteric wisdom.

With direct or indirect links with Freemasonry, many members of the ruling class became interested in spiritualism, occultism and in the wisdom of the East. The secretary of Count Cavour, Vincenzo Scarpa, founded the *Annali dello Spiritismo* (an important spiritualist journal); Giuseppe Mazzini was one of the first Italian apostles of reincarnation and Giuseppe Garibaldi (also a prominent Freemason) was involved in a number of movements of the occult underground and president of a spiritualist society. Members of the ruling class (and of Freemasonry) also founded the Italian branch of the Theosophical Society in 1898 and contributed to the spreading of Buddhism in Italy.

b) *The people* were largely Catholic and the nineteenth century saw a large growth in the popularity of folk devotion in the form of the cult of the Sacred Heart, of the Virgin Mary and of some saints, and also large pilgrimages. (In Italy apparitions of the Virgin Mary had long antedated Lourdes or La Salette: as early as 1432 the Virgin Mary had appeared in Caravaggio and still today 2.5 million people visit the Caravaggio shrine every year compared with 5.5 million pilgrims to Lourdes; there may have been even more in the nineteenth century.) We think that the importance of this 'religiosità popolare' (to be translated more with 'popular Catholicism' than with 'folk religion', since it was organized or at least controlled by the Church) should be particularly emphasized as a main feature of people's religion in the Monarchy of Italy.

The Church and the ruling class fought two main cultural battles during the Monarchy years:

i) *The struggle for the young*: the very strong educational institutions of the Church, serving both the rich (and the sons of the ruling class itself) and the poor competed with the state and its schools.

ii) *The struggle for the poor*: the Church with its huge charities soon won the battle with the State (who practically abandoned the poor to the care of the Church), only to find a stronger competitor in the socialists and, in our century, in the communist movement.

We have not discussed the Protestants in the Monarchy of Italy: their presence was minimal, apart from the Waldensians (pre-Reformation Protestants), and largely confined to their Northern valleys. The Waldensian myth was strong abroad, and the myth has a connection with the first missions of some Christian 'sects' to Italy. In the mind of the founding fathers of a number of 'sects', it should have been comparatively easy to convert the brave Waldensians, the oldest of all Protestants, to a new fullness of the Reformation. Accordingly, Joseph Smith, the Mormon prophet, suggested establishing a Mormon mission (which, after Smith's death, was in fact organized and led by apostle Lorenzo Snow) to visit the Waldensians in their valleys. Later, Ellen G. White, the prophetess of the Seventh-Day Adventists, John Nelson Darby (the father of Fundamentalism) and Pastor Charles T. Russell (the creator of the movement subsequently called Jehovah's Witnesses) visited the Waldensian valleys personally. They met with little success: notwithstanding the myth, the Waldensians were a closely tied community and far from eager to join any 'new religion'. However, the interest in the Waldensians led groups such as the Mormons and the Jehovah's Witnesses to develop their first interest in Italy. The seed they planted was destined to grow, if not among the Waldensians, among a certain percentage of the Catholic people.

The Republic (1946 to the present)

The main changes of the religious scenario after World War II have been as follows:

a) Despite the leading rule of the Christian Democrat Party in the government, a common conclusion of historians and sociologists has been that the ruling class in the cultural and economic fields, and in the education controlled by the state, and in the press, remains mostly non-Catholic or hostile to the Church. A minor development — however important for our purposes — is the 'democratization' of the interest in esoteric and occult themes, promoted by the ruling class but now also widespread among the people, where it has allied itself with an old interest for astrology and magic.

b) An internal migration of biblical proportions after World War II has moved an enormous number of Italians from the poorer south to the richer north in order to build an internationally powerful industry. An upward mobility has resulted in a willingness by many to adopt the values of the ruling class; as a result, popular Catholicism has largely declined and the Catholic Church (also due to some theological suspicions about popular devotions) has underestimated the importance of this popular religion for large parts of the Italian people.

c) In the 50s and the 60s the Church finally lost the struggle for the poor — also due to the decline of popular Catholicism, to its real competitor: the powerful Communist Party, which became a sort of religious affiliation (or dream) for millions.

d) The 'anni di piombo' ('leaden' or 'bullet' years, 1968-78) saw the emergency of a youth counterculture which developed in some fringes into terrorism; the country was shaken and shocked. Although terrorism was finally defeated, many values were lost as casualties in that war and even the Communist Party proved incapable of managing the situation.

e) Years after, the decline of the communist dream proved to be final, with recent international events being the final blow. The party, however, with a new name, has managed to survive (and even grow), among the recent waves of corruption scandals (while new populist parties, such as the League, have emerged), but the quasi-religious dream has been lost.

f) Particularly in the universities, the struggle for the young is not yet lost for the Church. In the 70s and the 80s a number of Catholic groups (called in Italy 'i movimenti', 'the movements') enrolled millions of youth, serving the conservatives as well as the liberals (from Comunione e Liberazione to the Neo-Catecumenali). Thanks to this group Italian Catholicism exhibits some unique features with respect to all other European countries:

i) According to 1989 and 1996 surveys, Italy's population is comprised of 30% to 33% active Roman Catholics (97% of Italians have been baptized in the Catholic Church); roughly 38% of these active Catholics are young, i.e. under 34.

ii) According to another survey, if the most active Catholics are divided in groups according to age, the most important group is from 18 to 29 years old.

iii) The same sources indicate that 70.4% of active Catholics are from the middle class or the upper classes.

The conclusion seems to be clear: youth from middle and upper classes are more likely to be active Catholics in Italy than middle-aged workers; the young are comparatively more active in the Church than middle-aged or older people and middle or upper class people are more active than the Italian lower classes. This Italian peculiarity has already been the subject matter of a number of sociological studies. The Catholic 'movements' are not the only reason for this phenomenon, but are an important part of the picture.

The targets of the 'sects' and new religious movements

Newcomers in a picture largely dominated by the conflict between the Catholic Church and the ruling class, the 'sects' and new religious movements, have targeted three main models of potential converts:

a) *The executive*: the member of the ruling class with few or no attachments to the Catholic Church, probably with anti-clerical feelings and with a class folklore including a traditional interest in occult and esoteric teachings.

b) *The university student*: the young from the middle or upper class, with a medium to high degree of culture, with some interest in religion and open to new spiritual experiences.

c) *The plebeian*: the lower factory worker, the elderly living on a small income, the small shopkeeper impoverished by the large distribution outlets, the southern immigrant to the north not yet accepted in the social fabric of the new town. The 'plebeian' is not necessarily poor, or very poor, but tends to regard himself as low on the social scale.

These three models of course are mere ideal types and do not represent the whole spectrum of the society, but seems to indicate the target of 'sects' and new religious movements. Not all movements, however, target all three models.

a) The Theosophical Society targeted the executive (or his wife) and the modern executive is still targeted by 'fashionable' Eastern groups: 'mainline' Buddhism (groups part of the European Buddhist Union, UBE) now even more fashionable after the success of the 1993 movie *Little Buddha* by Italian director Bernardo Bertolucci, Soka Gakkai, groups born in a theosophical milieu (Anthroposophy, Agni Yoga), and Transcendental Meditation. The executive is also targeted by the less 'democratized' occult-esoteric groups.

b) The university student is targeted by the new religious movements: the Unification Church, Scientology, the Rajneesh movement, the Sai Baba group, the Hare Krishna (all these groups also convert outside the university, but largely focus on this ideal model of convert).

c) The plebeian is the target of Jehovah's Witnesses, the Neo-Apostolic Church and the Mormons. However they are also targeted by the new Pentecostal Protestantism (the Assemblies of God have a following of almost 200,000 in Italy), by a fringe Catholicism (popular Catholicism with a tendency to fall outside the control of the Church: apparitions not recognized by the Church, healers, etc.) and by 'democratized' or plebeian forms of occultism and spiritualism.

If we look at the results, we find the following:

a) The groups targeting the executives rise and fall at the fringes of a class religious folklore shaped by an old interest in the occult and in the East: very few of them involve more than 1,000 people (Soka Gakkai, mainline Buddhism and perhaps Transcendental Meditation: the latter claims 20,000 'initiations' in Italy but only a small minority keeps up contact).

b) The 'classic' new religious movement is normally a failure in Italy in sociological terms: the Unification Church is reduced to less than 300 full-time members in Italy (and never had more than 600), the real 'members' of Scientology are less than 5,000, the Krishna devotees 300; the late Rajneesh and Sai Baba have more devotees but probably no new religious movement of this group can reach a figure in excess of 5,000 members in Italy (they speak, of course, of thousands of 'friends' or people in their mailing lists; in the case of Scientology 50,000 people may have had *some* contact with the group but this in most cases only means participating in a single meeting or visiting a centre with no subsequent involvement).

c) The 'plebeian' movements — or some of them — are *very* successful in Italy: Jehovah's Witnesses are the second Italian religion and the Mormons, having re-opened their Italian mission only in 1966, had a respectable membership of 18,000 in 1996. Still *more* successful, however, is 'fringe Catholicism'. Pilgrimages to Medjugorie,in Herzegovina,where the Virgin Mary allegedly appears, have been officially discouraged by the Italian Catholic Bishops (pending an examination by the Church of this rather controversial phenomenon). However, between 1.5 to 2 million Italian pilgrims visited Medjugorie in 1988. The number has since decreased because of the war in Bosnia, but huge Medjugorie gatherings are organized in Italy. Medjugorie pilgrims could not be classified as a new religious movement but often tend to separate themselves from the larger Catholic community and their attitude is unpredictable should the Catholic authorities conclude that 'their' apparition should not be 'recognized'. Outside mainline Catholicism are dozens of apparitions of the Virgin Mary explicitly declared as not genuine or even against the orthodox faith by the Catholic Church. It is not difficult for such groups to attract thousands of followers to their meetings, even if only a few of these followers would be prepared to break any relation with the Church. 'Democratized' occultism has been successful in creating a milieu, but not very successful in organizing it: while lecturers entering the circuit of esoteric-occult clubs and meetings (often connected to some bookshops) may easily raise an audience of hundreds or more in the larger cities, Rosicrucian and other ancient wisdom movements do not usually have a very large membership.

Sometimes, 'fringe Catholicism', plebeian occultism and new religious movements interact: an interesting case is the group called 'Nonsiamosoli' (We are not alone), headquartered in Porto Sant'Elpidio (Marche), born of a group called Fratellanza Cosmica (Cosmic Brotherhood) started by a UFO contactee, Eugenio Siragusa, in 1962, shutting down in 1978. The declining movement was revitalized in 1989, when the Virgin Mary of Fatima appeared to its new leader, Giorgio Bongiovanni, confirming that the mes - sages brought to Siragusa by the extraterrestrials were genuine. Bongiovanni (recognized in turn by the old Siragusa) has attracted a new following (more than 1,000 people in a few years) for *Nonsiamosoli*, and the group is again spreading abroad. An interesting point is that the themes come from the UFO contactee mythology (the familiar name of Ashtar Sheran is repeated) but also from 'fringe Catholicism' (the third secret of Fatima) and from plebeian occultism (Siragusa is introduced as a reincarnation, among others, of an ancient priest from Atlantis, of Cagliostro and of Rasputin: all popular folk heros in the cheap literature of popular occultism). To show as far the interaction may go, one of the former leaders of Siragusa's Cosmic Brotherhood — Roberto Negrini — was, at the same time, the importer into Italy of one of the branches of the esoteric order OTO, once led by Aleister Crowley, and the first Italian translator of Crowley's *Book of the*

Law (Negrini is no longer in contact with *Nonsiamosoli* or Siragusa at present).

Some groups target different social groups. Scientology is on the border between 'executives' and 'university students', but some local leaders considered a more 'democratic' approach to 'plebeians'. The Unification Church, when unsuccessful with the 'university students', seriously tried an approach to the 'plebeians' and gained some (not many) converts at the lower end of the social scale. The most 'interclass' groups, all comparatively small but growing, are Damanhur, Universal Life and Sukyo Mahikari (each probably approaching 1,000 committed followers, but having approached, or counted as members for a time, around 3,000). The reason for this is probably that — although Damanhur is a magical-esoteric community, Universal Life introduces itself as Christian and Sukyo Mahikari is one of the many new religions of Japan — all have in common an interest in the spirit world and in reincarnation and could attract followers both in the non-democratized and in the democratized traditions having something to do with spiritualism and reincarnation. For different reasons the Gnostic Movement founded by Colombian Samael Aun Weor (or rather its three branches, divided by subsequent schisms after the founder's death) attracts many around a blend of occultism, Rosicrucianism and sex magic.

Although further statistical work needs to be done, our preliminary conclusion is that there is a probable connection between the sociological situation of Catholicism and the success or failure of its competitors. The groups usually referred to as new religious movements have a difficult time in Italy because they have so far targeted mostly the 'university student', a model in our scheme indicating the young with high school or university education and of a social position from middle to high class. As mentioned earlier, many of these young adults with religious interests are kept within the Catholic Church (mostly by the Catholic 'movements') and are statistically a very relevant part of the community of practising or active Catholics; others probably have no religious or spiritual interest at all. Some Eastern groups have however attracted a fringe of the 'counterculture' of the 1960s and 1970s. A former leader of the Hare Krishnas, G. Cerquetti, was a contributor to the daily newspaper *Il Manifesto* (at the left of the Communist Party) and Andrea Valcarenghi, now a Rajneesh leader, was the editor of the underground/counterculture monthly

Re Nudo; Sai Baba followers' leader Antonio Craxi, brother of the former secretary of the Socialist Party and former Prime Minister Bettino Craxi, also comes from the counterculture. The groups targeting the 'executive', a model indicating members of the ruling class, have moderate success: the ruling class is traditionally not Catholic and remains also unchurched, although with a widespread vague spiritual (or occult) interest and mixed religious fascinations from a mythical Protestantism to Buddhism.

On the other hand, some of the groups targeting the 'plebeian' have achieved impressive results and have boomed in the last decade: this seems to be consistent with the conclusion that the Catholic Church has largely lost the struggle for the poor and its secular competitor, Communism, has also declined in recent years. The poor, however, remember the past strength of popular Catholicism and may still be attracted — still more than by Jehovah's Witnesses — by a 'fringe Catholicism' increasingly outside the control of the Church. Even the only real messianic movement of nineteenth century Italy, David Lazzaretti's Chiesa Giurisdavidica (which still has a few followers), has been interpreted by historians as a social protest in disguise or as a result of the fascination with Protestantism; new studies however, are increasingly proving that its background and followers came rather from 'fringe Catholicism'. Since two centuries of 'democratization' of spiritualism and the occult have also had their results, groups insisting on themes familiar to both 'fringe Catholicism' and plebeian occultism (like *Nonsiamosoli* and others) may perhaps grow in the future.

A final general comment is that media interest and public concern about 'the danger of cults' (or rather, in Italy, 'sects') is not proportionate with the real dimensions of the phenomenon.The anti-cult attitude of a majority of the press and of some political and religious forces seems to be an import from abroad if not an unreasonable reaction against the new and the strange. But the groups targeted by the anti-cult reaction — 'Moonies', Hare Krishna, Scientology — despite being very visible, only count a few hundred real followers. This is so true that no anti-cult organization can survive without finding itself devoting a large part of its time and resources to Jehovah's Witnesses. The only Italian anti-cult organization looking favourably to deprogram-ming and in touch with similar French, British and US organizations, ARIS (which never had more than a few dozen committed members and a mailing list of less than 1,000), was born as an anti-Scientology movement but survives only because, as its leaders have confirmed, around 80% of its time and resources are devoted to anti-Jehovah's Witnesses activities. If this is true of a nonsectarian organization like ARIS, it is still more true of the much larger Catholic cult-watching groups whose aims are largely connected with the Catholic concern for the growth of Jehovah's Witnesses.

The immigration to Italy of a large number of blacks and people from Third World countries has not changed the picture very much. The majority of these immigrants are Muslims and only a few dozen people attend the services of some Nigerian and other African new religions that reached Italy with black immigrants. They have no Italian converts, while the Iglesia ni Cristo from the Philippines has won a handful of Italian converts but still has no more than 200-300 followers in Italy, 90% of them immigrants from the Philippines.

A list of the main new religious movements in Italy

Method

In order to give a list of the main new religious movements active today in Italy, we have adopted a distinction between *new religious movements* and *new magical movements*. In both cases, we have taken into account only *movements* with some organization and structure and not single practitioners or authors of popular books who do not really 'organize' their readers or followers. We have, on the other hand, following Mircea Eliade, Julien Ries and others, regarded the *religious* experience and the *magical* experience as basically different. In the religious experience one looks for the sacred *per se*, and maintains a certain gratuity and reverence in his or her attitude. It is the rule (with some exceptions) that the religious experience looks for the supreme category of the Divine — be it called God or otherwise. On the other hand, the magical experience looks for the sacred as a tool capable of being dominated and manipulated by man for mundane purposes (sometimes 'high' such as ascending to a higher level of consciousness, but often 'low', such as increasing the magus' power and even money). The sacred is certainly regarded as higher than man even by the magus, but the magical experience as a rule does not regard an enquiry on the nature of the Divine as very important; a contact with superhuman 'entities' capable of helping the magus to achieve his aims is generally regarded as sufficient. Magic, of course, has always existed; but only from the 18th century (perhaps in some countries from one or two centuries before) *magical movements* with an organization and a structure have emerged. Hence the interest of the category of *new magical movements* as counterparts of the new religious movements within the general frame of the 'new religiosity'. We will examine the situation in Italy first of the *new religious movements* (a *conventional* term including both Christian 'sects' and the so called 'new cults') and then of the *new magical movements*.

New religious movements

This report makes use of a typology, current in Italy, based on the distinction between: (i) Christian 'sects' (groups of Christian *origin*, whether or not they may be theologically regarded as Christian); (ii) Eastern movements imported into Europe; (iii) movements 'invented' in the West. We are not including here — according to this volume's general project — Evangelical, Fundamentalist (including International Churches of Christ) and Pentecostal groups, although Italian scholars sometimes include them in their list of 'new religious movements'.

Christian 'sects'

We will follow a seven-group typology (according to Massimo Introvigne, *Le nuove religioni*, Milan: SugarCo, 1989) and detail what exists in Italy within each group:

a) *Direct heirs of the 'Radical Reformation'* (Anabaptists, Hutterites and the like): the only presences in Italy are some small groups of friends of the *Neo-hutterite* movement founded by Eberhard Arnold (and now re-entering Germany from the U.S. and England), and small *Unitarian Universalist* groups in Parma, Reggio Emilia and Sicily (normally connected with masonic lodges, who support also 'Friends of the Friends' groups interested in studying Quakerism in various cities).

b) *'Metaphysical' groups*: *Christian Science* has three churches (Milan, Rome, Florence) and two societies (Turin, Aosta). The only movement of the New Thought group with a small presence in Italy is *Unity School of Christianity*; the Swedenborgian *New Church* ('metaphysic' in another sense) was more important in the past century and is reduced to a couple of small groups.

c) *'Restitutionist' groups* (inspired by the idea of a 'restitution' of the original Church); the Utah *Mormons* have (1996) 18,000 members in Italy since re-opening their mission in 1966 (a nineteenth-century mission, one of the first in a non-English speaking country was discontinued after the emigration of some 80 converts from the Waldensian valleys to Utah). Among the minority Mormon splinter groups only the *Bickertonites* maintain a mission in Italy with around 60 active members. The *Catholic Apostolic Church* still maintains two congregations in Italy, but it is oversized by the growing *Neo-Apostolic Church* which claims 3,000 members (mostly in the north). Although William Darby preached personally in Italy the 'strict' *Brethren* are a minority in Italy; more important are the 'liberal' Brethren called *Assemblee dei Fratelli* who are also heirs to the 19th century *Chiese Cristiane Libere* of Pietro Guicciardini and Teodorico Pietrocola Rossetti (not to be confused with the anticlerical, politically liberal and short-lived *Chiesa Cristiana Libera* of Garibaldi's friend Alessandro Gavazzi).

d) *Adventist groups*: *Seventh-Day Adventists* have some 5,000 active members, introduced in Italy in the nineteenth century by Michat Belina Czechowski (their schism, the *Reform Movement*, also has a small presence in Italy). *Jehovah's Witnesses* are by far the largest non-Catholic group in Italy, with more than 200,000 active members and a community of around 400,000 (some of their schisms are also present: Alexander Freytag's schism, *Chiesa del Regno di Dio* with some 2,000 people, and the smaller *Chiesa Cristiana Millenarista* and *Berean Bible Students*). The *Worldwide Church of God* is small (probably less than 300) but was well-known for the very large free distribution of the Italian edition of its (now defunct) magazine *The Plain Truth* and for its radio and TV evangelical activities.

e) *Prophetic and messianic movements*: our typology would distinguish between *prophet* (announcing God) and *messiah* (a divine figure himself). The largest prophetic movements are the German-born *Vita Universale* (Universal Life) of prophetess-medium Gabriele Wittek (around 1,000 members and an active proselytism particularly in the greater Milan area) and *The Family* (tracing its origins to the Children of God). It no longer operates underground (after a long trial at the Court of Rome ended in 1991 with the acquittal of their Italian leaders), but is still difficult to evaluate its size (probably reduced to less than 50 members, since most Italians members now serve as missionaries in Eastern Europe). Messiahs, in a Christian context, would be defined for their relation to *the* Christian Messiah, Jesus Christ. They could pretend to be his 'second advent' or embodiment: such claims are made for the founders of both the *Unification Church* of the Reverend Moon (less than 300 members in Italy and now returning to proselytism after a greater emphasis on 'front' political or cultural organizations and groups of Unification origins like CAUSA) and the *Grail Movement* of Abd-ru-shin (small in Italy but now slowly growing).

Messiahs could also introduce themselves as a new incarnation of the Christ (a 'ri-incarnation' rather than a reincarnation): the Brazilian *SOUST* (Sovereign Universal Order of the Holy Trinity), with a handful of followers in Italy, so introduces its founder called 'Inri Cristo'. Another kind of Messiah could pretend to be a new incarnation in the divine family. The nineteenth century produced the famous case of David Lazzaretti, the prophet of Mount Amiata in Tuscany, born in 1834 and killed by the police in 1878. A group of his *Chiesa Giurisdavidica* still exists in his native Arcidosso, with some hundreds of people still loyal to the doctrine of Lazzaretti, while in Rome a smaller group (arising from the widow of a married Catholic priest who followed Lazzaretti and then died in Rome) has separated itself from the church in Arcidosso and, with the name of *Chiesa Universale Giuris-Davidica*, believes one of its leaders, Elvira Giro, to be the incarnation of the Holy Spirit. The latter small splinter group in Rome combines Lazzarettism with occultist themes and even belief in UFOs. Finally, a Messiah could be believed to be nothing less than God the Father himself. Two famous God-Messiahs, Father Divine and Georges Roux of Montfavet, never had a sizeable following in Italy; another, the Dutch fisherman Louwrens Voorthuizen ('Lou', 1898-1968), attracted some interest in Italy and a small *Lou Group*, headquartered in Turin, is still active and proselytizing. Yvonne Trubert's *IVI*, a prophetic-healing group not easy to classify, has a significant activity in Italy.

Finally, it is rather important to note a loose network of local prophets and apparitions of the Virgin Mary or of Jesus Christ not approved by the bishops. These religious movements have few printed documents and are not easy to know but their presence is growing in almost every Italian dioceses. The only groups with a nation-wide presence among this 'fringe Catholicism' are the *Apostoli della Fede* (Apostles of the Faith), founded in Rome by Basilio Roncaccia and active mostly in the Venitian area, and the *Church of the Universal Soul*, formerly *Chiesa della Nuova Gerusalemme* (Church of the New Jerusalem), founded in Turin by Roberto Casarin as 'Associazione Cristo nell'Uomo' (Association Christ in the Man), who adopted the new name after breaking with the Catholic Church and introducing Eastern teachings such as the Tao and reincarnation. The case of Casarin's Church shows how 'fringe Catholicism' could produce new religious movements separated from the Catholic Church.

f) *Schisms of Roman Catholic or Eastern Orthodox origin*: a category now more important after the schism of Mgr. Marcel Lefebvre's *Fraternity of St. Pius X*, not particularly successful in Italy (4-5 priests and less than 500 followers; the main conservative Catholic groups had abandoned Mgr. Lefebvre well before the schism); a 'sedevacantist' schism (i.e. a group arguing that the Holy See is vacant and John Paul II is not a 'real' Pope) a spin-off from Mgr. Lefebvre's movement, the *Istituto Mater Boni Consilii*, headquartered in Verrua Savoia (Turin) no longer has a bishop (one was consecrated by the sedevacantist bishop Guérard des Lauriers in France but subsequently left the group), but maintains a handful of priests, a small seminary and some 100 followers in various Italian cities. Still more extreme is the *Associazione Maria 'Salus Populi Romani'* of Turin, whose leaders — Stefano Filiberto and Gianluca Givogre — argue that a new Pope should be elected by 'sedevacantists' in the near future. They publish a newsletter *Il Nuovo Osservatore Cattolico*. A group of followers of the late 'antipope' Clemens XV of Clémery (France) has established the *Magnificat Group* near Brescia: the group includes references to UFOs and magic, has around 100 members and was attacked in 1991 in a pastoral letter of the Catholic Bishop of Brescia. Some *episcopi vagantes*, 'wandering bishops', with illicit but ostensibly valid orders appear from time to time in Italy (and are sometimes arrested, accused of impersonating a Roman Catholic bishop for fraudulent purposes).

More relevant are the links of a small but aggressive number of Catholic priests who have broken ties for different reasons with their Bishops, establishing Eastern churches apparently ready to distribute episcopal consecrations to doubtful candidates, like the prechalcedonian *Nestorian Church* (an Italian branch, *Chiesa Assira dell'Est*, with a bishop in the Venetian area, which later evolved into a parish of the *Polish Orthodox Autocephalic Church*) and the Greek *Old Calendarist Church* (Eastern Orthodox rejecting the new calendar). An Italian branch is headquartered in Sardinia with one bishop, Mgr. Giovanni Basciu and nine or ten priests; a separate *Holy Orthodox Church of Italy*, headquartered in Aprilia, near Rome, has been chartered by a different Old Calendarist Synod from Greece. Although the wandering bishops often style themselves as 'Old Catholics', the genuine Old Catholic Union of Utrecht has only a very small, almost symbolic mission (called *Missione Crist-cattolica*) formerly in Milan and now in Scandiano (Reggio Emilia).

g) *Syncretistic movements* of the Third World have been imported into Italy by foreign workers (such is the case with the *Rasta-farians)*; they are very small, with few attempts to proselytize among Italians, and with few results: such is the case with the *Iglesia ni Cristo* of the Philippines and the *Eternal Order of Cherubim and Seraphim* of Nigeria. The bizarre ultra-conservative Japanese group *Seibo no Mikuni* combining elements of Japanese folk religion and Catholic 'sedevacantism' also attempts to proselytize in Italy among people of Mgr. Lefebvre's milieu.

Eastern new religious movements

A typology could be established according to the 'great' religion where the different groups find their origin:

a) *Groups born in an Islamic milieu* are active in Italy: The *Baha'i* have a very old tradition and a significant cultural presence (although they do not number more than 300 people); other groups probably have less than 100 members. The *Ahmadis* are just starting to enter Italy; *Subud* is not very visible, but attract followers in the New Age milieu; and the syncretic *Daheshism* of Lebanon is being introduced through the growing Lebanese community in our country.

b) *Western groups looking to the East* grew out of the very old presence of the *Theosophical Society*; almost moribund, it has been revived by a renewed interest in Blavatsky and her esotericism in New Age circles; the Californian schism *Universal Lodge of Theosophists* (LUT) is probably more active than the Society; all the groups in the theosophical tradition (Alice Bailey's *Lucis Trust*; the *Krishnamurti* groups; *Anthroposophy*, with its respected Waldorf schools; Omraam Mikhaël Aivanhov's *Universal White Brotherhood*; the *I AM Religious Activity* and Helena Roerich's *Agni Yoga*) each have from some dozens to some hundreds of followers in Italy. Italy has shown a recent interest (still difficult to evaluate) in 'white guru' movements such as *Eckankar* and the *Johannine Daist Communion* of the eclectic Master Da Free John, and has also contributed its own Eastern-New Age group (actually one of the largest in Europe), *Damanhur*, founded by Oberto Airaudi and headquartered in a 300-person community in Baldissero Canavese (Turin) and with another 300 members in nearby 'satellite' communes and around 1,000 members at large, using Egyptian-occult symbolism but also theosophical influences. A huge underground temple — and a smaller temple above ground — has attracted considerable media attention. Other Northern Italian groups with theosophical roots include: *Helios Adeva*, created by Valerio Sanfo; *Asclepios*, whose leader is Aldo Del Negro and the *Ordine dei Maestri Shan*, a group somewhat similar to Eckankar with 50 followers in Turin. Two Italians also claim to be divine Avatars: Guglielmo Marino in Ponte Chiasso, near the Swiss border, with a curious blend of occultism and anti-Jewish themes; and Francesco Isa Atmananda ('Babaji') in Rome and Milan, whose recent 'Seventh Gospel' ('read it seven times and you will become God') has won some hundreds of converts (in Italy and abroad) to his *Associazione Mondiale La Rosa di Babaji*. The theosophically-oriented *Liberal Catholic Church* has two priests in Italy; one of them conducts Sunday services at the *Villaggio Verde* ('Green Village') in Cavallirio (Novara) created by Bernardino Del Boca as a commune for a few families and a week-end meeting point for many different theosophical and New Age groups. In the same area — with no direct links with the Green Village — one can find the independent *Gruppo Teosofico Sarmoung*.

c) *Eastern missions to the West* have been successful in Italy to a limited extent: *Hare Krishna* (headquartered in a monastery near

Florence) claim 300 full-time members and 50,000 'followers' (a figure probably indicating a mailing list); *Transcendental Meditation* has had 20,000 people in its courses (few stay) and maintains 25 centres; the *Rajneesh Movement*, with all its legal problems, claims 6,000 devotees in Italy but probably has around 800 (some teach 'hippotherapy': curing illnesses through horse-riding); older masters such as *Aurobindo* (whose followers are being out-numbered by those of his independent disciple *Sri Chinmoy*) and *Ramana Maharshi* still find a following of dozens in Italy; *Paramahansa Yogananda*'s books are very popular, but his followers are divided into a number of very small groups. Recently other groups such as *Brahma Kumaris* and *Ananda Marga* have entered Italy, but they are still small (less than 100 members). A larger success has been achieved by Sri Mataji Nirmala Devi's *Sahaya Yoga*, which has an *ashram* at Garlate (near Milan) and another near Rome, and the *Haidakhandi Samaji* devoted to the cult of the mythical avatar Babaji (with centres in Milan; Villa San Secondo, in the province of Asti; Cisternino, in the province of Brindisi; and Novara), both with 200-300 members. There are also *Radhasoami* groups such as *Kirpal Singh's* in Italy, while — arising from the same tradition but with unique features — *Élan Vital* (one called Divine Light Mission) has declined in Italy as in many other countries. Two groups with a Sikh origin also have a couple of hundred followers: *3HO* (with a centre in Rome) and the *Centro di Filosofia Acquariana* (Centre for Aquarian Philosophy) with centres in Milan and Albiano, Lucca, established in 1978 by Baba Bedi, a relative of the well-known movie actor Kabir Bedi. The largest guru or neo-Indian group in Italy is probably the *Sathya Sai Baba* movement. It has occasionally claimed 50,000 Italian devotees but this is probably only the size of its mailing list; however, there are around 1,000 Italian followers of this Indian 'miracle man'; as mentioned earlier, one of the movement's top leaders is Mr Antonio Craxi, brother of former Italian Socialist Party's leader Bettino Craxi (a fact often noted by the press). Another leader is Mario Mazzoleni, a former Roman Catholic priest excommunicated in 1992 for his role in Sai's movement and for his teachings on the divinity of Sai and on reincarnation. With the exception of Sathya Sai Baba's group, all neo-Indian movements appear to be declining in influence and size in Italy.

d) More than twenty *Buddhist* centres exist in Italy, particularly (but not only) in the Zen and Tibetan tradition; one of the most important is the *Istituto Lama Tsong Khapa* of Pomaia, in Tuscany, while the *Merigar* community of Tibetan monk Namkhai Norbu (also in Tuscany) with its peculiar Dzog-chen has also attracted people with magical and occult interests. The election in 1987 of an Italian, Mr Bruno Portigliatti, as president of the European Buddhist Union, confirmed the progress of Buddhism in Italy. Italian Buddhists (not including Soka Gakkai) probably number around 5,000, although higher figures (10,000 to 20,000) are occasionally claimed by Buddhist leaders.

e) Japanese new religions have also established some missions in Italy. Among the Japanese Buddhist groups, *Soka Gakkai* had an astonishing growth in the 1990s and now counts some 14,000 followers (including movie and sport stars), *Reiyukai* and *Ittio-en* both have a group in Milan, while *Rissho Kosei-kai* does not proselytize for Italian members and only has activities in the field of culture and dialogue with Christianity. Among the non-Buddhist groups, *Tenrikyo* — very important in Japan — has a single office in Rome, regarded only as a preliminary step for a future mission; *Cosmo Mate* has a handful of followers in Northern Italy. The most active Japanese new religion in Italy is *Sukyo Mahikari* (its competitor to the heritage of the founder Kotama Okada, Seiko Mahikari Bunmei Kyodan, never had an Italian group). Sukyo Mahikari has held more than 150 initiatory courses in Italy and has initiated some 3,000 people; around 1,000 are probably active. Its main centres are in Milan, Turin, Florence, Como, Peschiera del Garda, Bergamo, Varese, Brescia and Bari, with a small group in Rome. The success of Sukyo Mahikari in Italy is an amazing example of trans-culturality; one sees bank clerks or middle-class shop owners in Turin or Milan adopting such quintessentially Japanese customs as an ancestor altar or shrine at home where rice is offered daily to the souls of the ancestors.

f) *Mazdaznan*, a group whose purpose is to spread Zoroastrian teachings in the West, has always had followers in Italy and still has small groups in a number of cities; although its total membership does not reach 100, the ideas of its founder O.Z. Hanish on hygiene and diet have attracted the attention of some doctors.

Western new religious movements

Scientology is the most significant Western-born new religious movement in Italy. Its multiple claims of 50,000 to 500,000 'contacts' refer to people either on its mailing lists or having passed a preliminary 'personality test'. Probably some thousands of people have enrolled at least in one Scientology course; no more than 5,000 regard themselves as 'members' of the Church of Scientology. Scientology is probably the most controversial movement in Italy and has been discussed in a number of court cases. In 1991 the Court of Milan — reversing a preliminary ruling by Judge Mulliri — declared Scientology's operation *per se* legal in Italy and acquitted a number of leaders from the main charges filed against them; in 1993 the Court of Appeal of Milan partially reversed the first degree decision and found most of the Scientologists individually guilty of a number of charges (without outlawing Scientology as an organization). In 1995 the Supreme Court reversed in favour of Scientology the decision of the Court of Appeal of Milan. The latter (whose feud with the Supreme Court, largely political, goes well beyond Scientology) convicted again the same defendants in 1996 and a new recourse to the Supreme Court is now pending. In the meantime, in 1996 after a thirteen year battle, the Court of Turin — in a final decision, declared Scientology a bona fide religion in a case concerning its tax status. Among the splinters from Scientology, the *Advanced Ability Centre* is active in Milan. Other human potential movements include *Silva Mind Control* (with centres in Turin, Milan, Rome) and *Evo Cris*, a group originally established in Mexico which has borrowed a number of ideas from Silva. An older Western-born religion, the Belgian *Antoinism*, maintains two reading rooms in Milan and Postua (Vercelli).

New Magical Movements

We will follow the typology outlined in M. Introvigne, *Il cappello del mago* (Milan: SugarCo, 1990) and will only deal with organized movements, without discussing the considerable influence of esoteric authors such as Italian Julius Evola or French René Guénon who have not established 'structures' or movements.

Spiritualist groups

Although surveys have claimed that 10% to 15% of Italians have some belief in spiritualism, only a small number are members of organized spiritualist groups. The *Scuola Scientifica Basilio*, started in Argentina and with Italian headquarters in Florence, is probably the more organized of the mediumistic movements in Italy, with a following of around 200-300. Much less structured is the *Cerchio Firenze 77*, founded by the followers of Italian medium Roberto Setti (1930-84), but its literature is very popular in all spiritualist circles. A mediumistic healing group from France, *APRES* of Maguy Lebrun, has recently been quite active in Italy; although openly spiritualist and reincarnationist it tries to attract Catholics and takes advantage of the interest in communication with the dead, which undoubtedly also exists among the Catholics. A new spiritualism (where 'voices' from 'entities' not necessarily claiming to be the dead are heard) is reappearing in the New Age movement as 'channelling'. Books like *A Course in Miracles* and the texts of *Jane Roberts* and *Shirley MacLaine* are known in Italy and some New Age study groups meet to read them together. The most structured phenomenon in the channelling-New Age area is connected with the *Findhorn Foundation* which is organized and represented in Italy. It is interesting to note that some of the themes of the New Age (and of the method of channelling) were anticipated in Italy by Pietro Ubaldi (1886-1972), a former Catholic condemned by the Church in 1932 for his pantheist and reincarnationist ideas allegedly 'received' from the voice of God himself. His group, *Nucleo Ubaldiano di Metafisica*, popularly called *La Grande Sintesi* (from the title of his main book) has however a few followers in Italy, but many more in South America, particularly in Brazil.

UFO groups

Italy has not escaped the UFO fad (although a very popular 'ufologist', Renato Vesco, explained flying saucers as CIA or KGB spying devices), and the religious messages of the 'space brothers' have been heard in our country. As in other countries, the extraterrestrial called 'Ashtar Sheran' has spoken through a number of mediums in the north and in the south of Italy (it is interesting to note how the name 'Ashtar Sheran' returns in mediumistic messages from the outer space in different groups apparently with no connection, from Berlin to Belgium and from Spain to Italy). Italy was the home of *Centro Studi Fratellanza Cosmica* founded by the Sicilian Eugenio Siragusa (born 1919) in 1962 and discontinued in 1978; we have discussed in the first part of this paper the success of its continuation as *Nonsiamosoli*, combinating UFOs and the Virgin of Fatima. Nonsiamosoli is, if we exclude some attempt by Damanhur, the only Italian-born group proselytizing outside of Italy. Due to the recent revival Siragusa's movement could again dispute the title of largest Italian UFO group with the *Raelian Movement*, an atheistic-edonistic French-based group which has hundreds of followers in Italy (where a tour by founder Claude Vorilhon, 'Raël' in early 1989 attracted a considerable media interest).

'Fringe Masonry'

Although mainline Freemasonry is probably outside our field of study, such is not the case for what has been called 'Fringe Masonry' and includes para-masonic (or pseudo-masonic) groups and rites whose structure is masonic but whose interests are mainly magical and occult. These groups, particularly in Italy, although small, have proved to be a centre and a milieu where occultists of different persuasions meet. We would mention only the main family of 'Fringe Masonry', the 'Egyptian' rites of Misraim and Memphis. It is possible (although not certain) that their very origin is Italian and has something to do with the 'Egyptian masonry' organized by Cagliostro at the end of the eighteenth century. Be it as it may be, the rites of Misraim and Memphis (united or separated) have had — and to some extent still have — an important role in the world of the new magical movements. These rites have had many schisms; in Italy the main groups are the *Rito Antico e Primitivo di Memphis-Misraim* (once led by the Perugia doctor Francesco Brunelli, 1927-82, one of Italy's leading authorities on magic), the *Sovrano Santuario Adriatico* (once headed by Gastone Ventura, 1904-81, an important figure of the Italian magical milieu, and after his death in 1981 by Sebastiano Caracciolo) and the *Sovrano Santuario Mediterraneo* (a schism of the former) headed in Sicily by Gaspare Cannizzo. Other smaller splinter groups also exist.

Pythagorean orders

Orders claiming a mythical descent from Pythagoras have existed in Europe since at least the eighteenth century. In Italy such claims were held by Arturo Reghini (1878-1946), another important character of the magical milieu, well-known for his anti-Catholic tirades. A review called *Ignis,* edited by Roberto Sesti, in the south of Italy, has continued the ideas (and the strong anti-Catholic bias) of Reghini; it was apparently discontinued in 1994. Another Pythagorical order, the *OHTM* (Hermetic Order Tetramegystus and Mystical), originating in Belgium, is also present in Italy in the same groups interested in the rites of Misraim and Memphis. A 'Greek' philosophy is the main feature of the Argentinian movement *New Acropolis* (Nuova Acropoli), a group which strongly denies being a 'new religion' and styles itself as a 'philosophical school'. Its distinctive beliefs in fairies and similar beings (as well as in a new world order, different from the present Western democracy and closer to Plato's *Republic*) probably allows us to include Nuova Acropoli among the new magical movements, notwithstanding its obvious borrowings from Theosophy; it has some hundreds of followers in Italy and centres in various cities (while the other groups each have less than 100 — and probably less than 50 — members).

'Great Brotherhoods'

The idea of a 'great (universal) brotherhood of the initiates' is the main feature of a number of groups; usually they emphasize the need for world peace through a world government. In Italy both the main groups of this kind have a presence of some dozens of people (and larger mailing lists): the *Great Universal Brotherhood* (Grande Fraternità Universale) founded by Serge Raynaud de la Ferrière (present in Italy in its two separated branches) and the *International Biogenic Society* founded by Edmond Bordeaux Szekely. A similar indigenous group is the *Logos Centre*, headquartered in Cremona.

Rosicrucian orders

Not all the Rosicrucian orders are present in Italy. The largest Rosicrucian organization in Italy (as in the world at large) was the

AMORC with some thousands enrolled in the correspondence course and a number of centres. However, the recent internal troubles in the US (and the schism of a part of the French group) have had their effects. In Italy membership seems to be decreasing. As a consequence, the Dutch-based *Lectorium Rosicrucianum* now sees a chance to become the largest Rosicrucian group in Italy; its posters are often present in many Italian cities and the group is very active. The *Rosicrucian Association* of Max Heindel also exists in Italy (with the name *ARCO*) but is smaller than the other two groups. The *Fraternitas Rosicruciana Antiqua* of Arnoldo Krumm-Heller has a group in Milan connected with the *Gruppo Prometeo* (combining Krumm-Heller, Kremmerz and other occult masters with a political interest in communism; the leader is a former member of the Red Brigades), with about a dozen followers.

Martinist orders

Sometimes regarded as a variety of freemasonry, Martinism has its own distinctive place among the magical movements. Its history of schisms is particularly complicated: most of the intricacies depend on different trends arising from the more magically operative tradition of Martinez de Pasqually and the more mystical tradition of Louis-Claude de Saint-Martin. Also, in contemporary Italy the two main branches, the *Ordine Martinista* and the *Ordine Martinista Antico e Tradizionale* reflect the differences between a 'martinist' (Saint-Martin) and a 'martinezist' (Martinez de Pasqually) wing, the former once represented by Gastone Ventura and the latter by Francesco Brunelli, who disputed to Ventura a sort of general leadership of the Italian occult-magical orders. The division is now continued by their respective successors (Brunelli's group has between 100 and 200 followers, Ventura's around 50; a number of minor Martinist orders also exist).

Gnostic Churches and Movements

The various branches of the Gnostic Church founded in 1890 in Paris by Jules Doinel have existed and still exist in Italy. Vincenzo Soro before World War II and Giordano Gamberini immediately after the war helped the French Gnostic Church to spread in Italy (Gamberini subsequently became Great Master of the Grande Oriente, the larger Italian masonic body). Francesco Brunelli was also consecrated as a Gnostic bishop under a French line and a number of rival bishops presently claim his succession as head of the Italian Gnostic Church; the only one with a sizeable following is Loris Carlesi of Florence. His records mention 140 followers. Carlesi's *Italian Gnostic Church* is not without competitors: within some of the OTOs (see below) a Gnostic succession is also claimed. The larger gnostic bodies are probably the Gnostic Movement founded by the Colombian Samael Aun Weor (1917-77) present in Italy with its three main branches (one in Colombia and two in Mexico), which separated after the founder's death. The main centres are near Milan and in Novara.

OTO

OTO, the Ordo Templi Orientis, is one of the most important organizations of ceremonial magic of our century. Founded by Carl Kellner and Theodor Reuss, it became famous through Aleister Crowley. After Crowley's death, more than one hundred rival groups in the world have claimed OTO heritage (notwithstanding the very controversial nature of his sex magic teachings). The *'Caliphate' OTO* (recognized as the owner of the trademark OTO by a US court decision in 1985) has a seat in Rome and another in Northern Italy with some 100 followers. Among its schismatic competitors, two derived from the conglomerate of magical organizations founded by the American magus Michael Bertiaux, who — although mainly interested in his Gnostic Church — has operated an OTO, an OTOA (OTO 'Ancient'), as well as a rite of Memphis and Misraim and a number of other magical orders. In Italy Bertiaux gave a charter in 1978 to Nevio Viola of Trieste (Solomon-Phallos-Naos-Lucifer I). Viola then proceeded to organize an OTO in Italy and an external circle called *Corrente 93 — Società Pansophica per la Nuova Era* with centres — and reviews — in Trieste (*Abraxas*), Locri (*Sixtrum*) and Bergamo (*Studi Iniziatici*). In 1982 the Spaniard Manuel Lamparter (Tau Baphomet X) also appointed Viola as representative of OTOA in Italy (Bertiaux's charter covered only OTO). In 1983 Viola — having had some health problems — appointed Roberto Negrini of Bologna (Moloch-Solomon-Phallos-Naos-Lucifer II) as his successor as head of the following organizations in Italy: OTO, OTOA, Ecclesia Gnostica Catholica (Latina), Astrum Argentinum, by Couleuvre Noire (a voodoo organization founded by Bertiaux), Illuminati d'Italia, Fraternitas Rosicruciana Antiqua (not to be confused with the Milan group), while the 'Ancient and Primitive Rite of Memphis and Misraim' works were suspended with authorization to Negrini to start them again in the future (charter of September 25, 1988). Negrini is a flamboyant personality (on October 10 1989 he staged a sex magic performance — under the name of Roberto Lotario di Chiaravalle — for the popular TV network *Canale 5*), and the 'Corrente 93' group has experienced a number of schisms. In 1990 Viola himself tried to get back into the picture against Negrini, but Negrini regarded the 1988 charter as irrevocable and Bertiaux (who had retired from many of his OTO positions in favour of the Californian Courtney Willis) elected to stay out of the fight. At any rate 'Corrente 93' is no longer in existence with this name. Some of the Trieste members joined 'Frank G. Ripel' (a Mr Gianfranco Perilli), who operates the *Associazione Orion* and other groups and has written extensively on sex magic; in the south Giuseppe Ierace operates the *Società Psicofisica di Studi Metapsichici*. Being a clinical neuropsychiatrist, Ierace emphasized a psychoanalytical interpretation of Crowley. Negrini continues to operate a Gnostic Church, an OTO and an OTOA with perhaps one hundred members, and has also organized a *Draconian Order* with a mother abbey, 'Leviathan' in Rome, and a magazine called *Daimon*. He has recently declared his order 'international' and independent from Bertiaux. Not to be confused with other rock-music based groups connected with the different OTO, is the rock-Crowley, an English movement *TOPY* (Temple of Psychick Youth) which had a number or problems in Italy but is apparently still active.

Brotherhood of Miriam

An Italian-born magical tradition is the *Fratellanza di Miriam* (Brotherhood of Miriam, or Myriam) founded by Giuliano Kremmerz (pseudonym of Ciro Formisano, 1871-1930) an external circle of a more secret *Ordine Egizio* (where Kremmerz was not the main leader). Where the Brotherhood of Miriam only operated therapeutic magic and was a sort of school for healers, the Ordine Egizio also taught a system of sex magic claiming a link with the tradition established in Naples by Cagliostro and his circle. At least six contemporary different groups claim to be the 'genuine' heirs to Kremmerz; and almost all of these groups has its own

Ordine Egizio as the inner circle. Other groups (including the *Phoenix* in Naples and others) claim a link to a pre-Kremmerz 'Egyptian' tradition in Naples and in the south of Italy. Several hundred people are in touch with these groups, whose influence in the magic milieu is also felt outside the borders of Italy.

Neo-Templarism

The Templar myth is as popular in Italy as in other countries. The largest Italian group *Ordine Templare*, was passed on by Adolfo Banti to Gastone Ventura and is now in the hands of the heirs of Ventura (but not without schisms). Other neo-Templar groups of more recent origin also exist in connection with Swiss or Brazilian organizations, particularly in Rome (under Rocco Zingaro) and Turin (under Ferruccio Castoldi). These groups would like to be 'recognized' as 'legitimate' by the Catholic Church, but this is of course difficult in view of the roots of modern neo-Templarism in the occult and magical milieu. Media claims notwithstanding, the notorious Order of the Solar Temple was never active in Italy.

Gurdjieffian Groups

George Ivanovitch Gurdjieff's ideas are quite popular in the Italian occult milieu and are promoted by a number of celebrities, including folk singer Franco Battiato. A few international organizations (including the California-based *Fellowship of Friends* and the Scandinavian *Limbu Centre*) and a number of independent study groups are active in Italy. Many of the rival organizations object to the Fellowship of Friends' practice of visiting bookshops, inserting in books authored by Gurdjieff — often without the knowledge nor the authorization of the bookshop owners — fliers with telephone numbers of their 'Gurdjieff Ouspensky Centres' in a number of cities.

Neo-paganism and Wicca

The neo-pagan tradition known as *Wicca* in the US has been almost unknown in Italy until late 1993, when a meeting to promote it was held in a large Milan hotel. Only its feminist version had surfaced from time to time in the journals of the Italian feminist movement, but probably very few (if any) organized groups existed before 1993. On the other hand, *Druid* groups exist in Milan and in other cities; and recently a *neo-Roman* pagan movement (active during the first years of the fascist government) has surfaced again. The actual neo-Roman movement is as pagan as ever (they even celebrate pagan weddings in the name of the Roman god Janus) but tries to disassociate itself from the right-wing political groups and to be recognized as a genuine religion. It has two reviews (*Arthos* in Pontremoli, Tuscany, and *La Cittadella* in Messina, Sicily) and claims some 500 followers. While the main wing of the neo-Roman movement is monotheistic, in Milan art critic Antonino De Bono has founded the *Nuclei Neo-Ellenici di Religiosità Politeistica*, which is polytheistic and neo-Greek. The Nuclei have in Milan and in the Venitian region a couple of hundred followers and have attracted some press interest. Neo-pagan groups at times regard themselves as part of the 'New Age', but the label is also used (perhaps more appropriately) for theosophical groups like Damanhur or the Green Village and for a variety of business enterprises.

Satanism

The idea that Satanism has a very large following in Italy (and particularly in Turin) is largely a urban legend and a fabrication by the press (cheerfully confirmed by some Satanist leaders themselves). The often repeated figure of 40,000 Satanists in Turin alone cannot be substantiated by any evidence and was first mentioned by students at the University of Turin as an April Fool Day's hoax in 1950. Scholarly studies have concluded that the two rival *Churches of Satan* in Turin (established around 1970 following California models) each have less than 10 members. The largest Satanist groups in Italy are probably the *Confraternita of Efrem del Gatto* (Rome) and the *Bambini di Satana* ('Children of Satan', Bologna). The latter had 200 followers before police action, following charges of rape, in fact disrupted it in 1996. From time to time, teenage (and sometimes adult) groups engage in ritualistic activities of a satanic kind (profanation of cemeteries and churches, animal sacrifices, etc.) and are identified by the police; these groups — often influenced by some novels or by 'satanic' rock music — are normally very small and nothing supports the theory of a national network between them.

Cult controversies — Research and pastoral centres

The reaction to the new religious movements in Italy is different if one takes into account the Christian 'sects' and, respectively, all the other groups. The Catholic Church has been particularly concerned since World War I about the growth of some Christian 'sects' (including Pentecostalism, not discussed in this paper), and in many instances has focused its attention on one group only: Jehovah's Witnesses, by far the largest non-traditional religious group in Italy. On the other hand, the non-Catholic press and the majority of the political parties have normally regarded any anti-Jehovah's Witnesses attitude as a form of Catholic intolerance and have sided with the Witnesses in many instances, finally winning for them an official recognition as a religious organization. Other groups of Christian origin such as the Seventh-Day Adventists and (to a lesser extent) the Mormons, have found themselves in less controversial situations. In the 1970s with the growth of the Unification Church, the Hare Krishnas and Scientology, an anti-cult attitude has also surfaced in non-Catholic cultural and political groups, using the arguments of the international anti-cult movement (brainwashing, business operations disguised as religion, etc.). The 'new cults' have been defended by a part of the political left as fellow travellers of the counterculture (Rajneesh had been offered the position of president of the Radical Party). The anti-cult movement inclined towards deprogramming, and the request of new laws against the cults has never been very strong in Italy, emerging only in the 1980s and being characteristic of very minor organizations (*ARIS*, the construction of Monza businessmann Ennio Malatesta, is more 'activist' and favourable to deprogramming, while the *Studio dei culti emergenti* founded by the Rome lawyer and University professor Michele Del Re is more interested in scholarly activity and in introducing anti-cult legislation). Anti-cult movements are promoted by a part of the press and by some political parties but have very few ties with the Catholic community.

Catholic organizations are much larger, and although sometimes very concerned about the attitudes of groups like Scientology or the abrasive anti-Catholic propaganda of Jehovah's Witnesses, generally try to distance themselves from the small anti-cult lobby. *GRIS* (Gruppo di ricerca e di informazione sulle sette) is a pastoral group founded in 1983, authorized by the

Catholic Bishops' Conference and operating in the dioceses where the local bishop accepts the institution of a group, with a yearly national convention. It now covers many parts of Italy and acts as an umbrella organization coordinating most of the Catholic pastoral efforts in this field. *CESNUR* (Centre for Studies on New Religions), although founded and directed by Roman Catholics, has an international board of directors including a majority of non-Catholics, and is an international organization of scholars with no direct pastoral aims, whose purpose is to sponsor multi-disciplinary conferences and research projects, including academics of different religious persuasions and backgrounds.

The Roman Catholic Church has promulgated a number of recent documents, including the report *Sects and New Religious Movements* by the Secretariat for Ecumenism and Dialogue of the Bishops' Conference (May 30th, 1993), and the 100-page pastoral letter of March 6th, 1993, *New Religious Consciousness and New Evangelization* by Mgr. Giuseppe Casale, Archbishop of Foggia and president of the Italian branch of CESNUR. These documents criticize the anti-cult movement, rely largely on the scholarly surveys of the field and insist that the real challenge for the Roman Catholic Church in Italy is represented by a larger 'new religious consciousness' rather than by the new religious movements. The latter include among their members less than 1% of Italians, while belief in reincarnation (the most typical belief of the 'new religious consciousness') claims 25% of Italian adults and 35% of the high school students according to recent surveys. Within the general perspective of the 'new evangelization', suggested by Pope John Paul II, Italian Bishops see their problem, unlike anti-cultists, not a rising *membership* in the new religious movements but a rising *belief shopping* by the unchurched majority of the Italians and by the active Catholics themselves.

Appendix I

Summary of the Results of a Survey on Public Awareness of the New Religious Movements in Turin

Executed by: Studio Associato di Consulenza Aziendale, Lanzo Torinese (Turin)

Date: March, 1990

Sample: A sample of 100 in downtown Turin has been used, established as significant in previous market surveys. Gender, age and education have been balanced without targeting a special group. A control group has also been used (also in downtown Turin) with results confirming those of the principal sample. Downtown Turin is normally representative of the average Italian public; note however that the presence of Mormons is higher inTurin than in most other Italian cities.

1. Definitions

Understand the term	Yes (%)	No (%)
New Religions	25	75
New Religious Movements	10	90
Cults/New Cults	1	99
Sects	40	60

(Italian terms used: nuove religioni, nuovi movimenti religiosi, culti/nuovi culti, sette).

2. Reactions

Regards the sects/new religions/new religious movements as negative/ dangerous

Yes (%)	No (%)
80	20

3. Groups

Requested to mention a new religion/sect/new religious movement mentions (in percentage):

Jehovah's Witnesses	80
Mormons	13
Scientology	1

Note: The survey has been executed in March 1990, *before* the wider notoriety of Scientology arising from the Milan Court cases.

CHAPTER 6

New Religious Movements in Switzerland

Jean-François Mayer

Introduction

The frightening case of the Solar Temple[1] has brought to the world's attention that peaceful Switzerland, too, is a country where many religious movements are active. As in so many other countries in the West, the emergence of new religious movements in Switzerland during the past thirty years has aroused curiosity, questions, and sometimes anxiety. In order to get a more accurate picture of the current situation and its origin, we conducted an historical and sociological research from 1987 to 1990. Our research revealed the limitations of the phenomenon as far as numbers are concerned and the obvious broadening of answers available on the religious market. Actually, the situation in Switzerland looks quite similar to what one would find in other European countries; we could even suggest that Switzerland offers quite a representative synthesis of what is currently going on around Europe. The detailed results of our research have been published as a book, in which interested readers are able to find more material as well as chronological and statistical data.[2] This paper will confine itself to some observations of a general nature.

The religious situation in Switzerland

Diversity is the characteristic of Switzerland, which is a federal state constituted of 26 cantons and half-cantons. Each canton has its political, administrative and religious characteristics. The prevalence of four national languages only adds to this diversity. It should be observed here that religious borders are not similar to those between languages. There is a complex tangle of regional characteristics at various levels.

The Roman Catholic Church and the Reformed Church are the two main religious denominations in Switzerland. In 1980, 90% of the population still belonged to them, and their share was more or less the same, although the Roman Catholic Church had slightly more members, due to the huge presence of migrant workers coming from predominantly Roman Catholic Southern European countries. But the results of the 1990 census reveal that an important shift took place within ten years: while members of the Reformed Church still constituted 44.3% of the population in 1980, they only make up 39.98% in 1990; the percentage of Roman Catholics, on the other hand, remains relatively stable: 46.32% against 47.9% in 1980. Mainly in some of the larger towns, the number of people claiming no religious affiliation has grown dramatically, from 3.8% in 1980 to 7.4% in 1990. The city of Basel is probably the most extreme case: in this city, people without a religious affiliation have by now become the most important group: 35%, while 32% are Reformed and 25% Roman Catholic. In summary, the Roman Catholic Church and the Reformed Church are still holding their dominant position but not without new challenges, since a growing number of people are moving away from the established religious institutions.

The coexistence of two main Churches in Switzerland may seem to offer the image of religious harmony. Actually, it has become so only through a long historical evolution which has included many situations of conflict. As late as the nineteenth century, the birth of an Old Catholic movement (which in Switzerland is called 'Christian Catholic Church' and which now numbers no more than 12,000 members according to the 1990 census) was openly supported by the governments of several cantons in an attempt to weaken Roman Catholicism. A few years ago, projects in view of establishing new Roman Catholic bishoprics (for instance in Geneva) led to quite heated debates. Nevertheless, although some prejudices are more sustained than one would usually expect, it is true that the relationships between the two main denominations are, generally speaking, open and friendly.

With regard to the legal situation of religions, it is rather difficult to give an adequate summary in just a few lines. Louis Carlen comments:

The cantons are sovereign, insofar as their sovereignty is not limited by the Federal Constitution; in this way, the cantons are entitled to exercise all the competences which have not been transferred to the central authorities. Church law is part of that sovereignty. Most of the affairs relating to Church law are regulated by the cantons themselves. This explains why, on the basis of its own historical and religious background, each canton has developed different rules.[3]

As such, an adequate overview would then require a summary of 26 different canton statuses each containing their own characteristics, which would make it an impossible task within the frame of this paper. It is sufficient to say that the separation of Church and State is seen only in the cantons of Geneva and Neuchâtel (although in practice it is not an absolute separation), while, in most of the cantons, the Roman Catholic Church and the Reformed Church enjoy a public law status; such is also the case for the Christian Catholic Church in nine cantons, and for the Jewish community in four cantons. This public law status allows for church taxes, the payment of which is mandatory for people who have not officially left the Church. There is today a growing tendency towards a greater autonomy of the Churches, and revisions are being made in several cantons.

What is then the legal situation of those religious denominations which are not recognized? Augustin Macheret summarizes it this way:

All those religious communities which are not recognized have to follow the regulations of private law, within the boundaries of public order. Such is the status automatically ascribed to them, even if the laws of the canton do not mention it explicitly. In eight cantons (Bern, Jura, Nidwald, Obwald, Solothurn, Tessin, Valais, Fribourg), the cantonal constitutions allow the legislative power to grant such religious communities a public law status, if so desired. In four cantons (Fribourg, Jura, Tessin, Valais), such a recognition can intervene only if certain preconditions are fulfilled (the communities should have some importance at the cantonal level and/or have been active in the canton for a long period). In three cantons (Nidwald, Obwald, Solothurn), preconditions for a possible recognition are not given. The recently revised constitution of the canton of Bern entrusts the legislative power with the task to determine what the conditions should be.[4]

It may be of interest to know that in 1990 in the canton of Bern, following a referendum which had been launched by a conservative Christian political group, a bill for a cantonal law which could have entitled other religious communities which fulfilled certain preconditions (i.e. more than 500 members and more than 20 years of activity in the canton) to a public law status, was turned down by a clear voting majority. Several arguments were used by those who advocated a rejection of the bill. For instance, an important one was the fear of improving the situation mainly for Islam, but also for cults.

As to the tax situation, too, that differs from one canton to the next. Some non-recognized religious denominations obtain tax-exempt status in some cantons, while in other cantons they are thought of in the same way as any other association would be.

Historical roots of the new religious movements

As in other European countries, the wave of spiritualism reached Switzerland shortly after 1850. However, it did not lead to the creation of new religious movements in Switzerland, although there were some interesting developments. For instance, in 1853 at spiritualist sittings in Geneva, a table began to deliver teachings supposed to come from Christ himself, which resulted in the creation of a short-lived religious group.[5] But the content of the messages (a number of which were printed at that time) leaves the reader with the feeling that, had the group been able to survive, it would probably have become a pious Christian sect rather than a new religion. It was not until the twentieth century that a religious movement with spiritualist roots was born in Switzerland: the *Geistige Loge* (Spiritual Lodge) in Zurich, founded officially in 1948. It describes itself as Christian but is not without links with contemporary alternative religiosity[6] — as is the case with several other German-speaking movements, usually labelled *Neuoffenbarungen* ('new revelations') by German experts, which mix spiritualistic features with Christian themes (the latter are very often reinterpreted in accordance with the tastes of the cultic milieu).

Looking around for other forerunners of new religious movements in Switzerland, one is bound to meet the Theosophical Society, created in the United States in 1875, which very soon after left its spiritualistic background in order to answer the call from the East. Its historical significance, both in the development of modern occultism and in the interest in Eastern religions and philosophies, is well-known. The Swiss section of the Theosophical Society was founded in 1910, but there had been local lodges before that, affiliated either with the French Section (for instance in Geneva as early as 1901) or with the German Section. The creation of a Swiss Section took place because of the rivalry between Annie Besant and Rudolf Steiner; faithful to Besant, the four lodges then existing in Geneva subdivided into seven lodges which is the minimal number required to obtain a charter for a national section. This took place even though they mustered only 61 members, while 132 members followed Steiner (mainly in the German-speaking part of Switzerland, but also in Neuchâtel, as well as a group of Germans in Lugano).[7] As one can see, the membership remained limited, even if lumped together. The newly created Swiss Section at first enjoyed a rapid growth and in 1917 reached a high point of 364 members. However, in the following years, internal differences and quarrels weakened the section greatly. Although some theosophists were able to extend their sphere of influence,[8] it seems rather difficult to evaluate the impact of the Theosophical Society as a movement: its uninterrupted presence in Geneva since the beginning of the century (with a meeting hall and regular activities) has meant the spreading of certain doctrines, but this is of course difficult to measure precisely; and, anyway, the theosophical legacy in the alternative religiosity of today is a global phenomenon, not a specifically Swiss one.

Theosophy was not, even at that time, the only way for 'turning East'. There is little doubt that the kind of East introduced through the teachings of Mazdaznan, for instance, was somewhat mythical; Mazdaznan was (and remains) a strange mixture of occult teachings, Zoroastrianism, Christianity and Lebensreform. In 1907, Swiss-born David Ammann (1855-1923) was selected by Otoman Zar-Adusht Hanish (1844-1936) to become the emissary for the teachings of Mazdaznan in Europe. Ammann first settled in Leipzig, but travelled as early as 1911 with Hanish around Switzerland. Expelled from Germany in 1914, Ammann came to Switzerland on a permanent basis and developed an intense activity in the German-speaking part of the country. Later, a lot was done from Geneva for the spreading of the movement in the French-speaking area through the work of Pierre Martin (d.1949), who translated the teachings of Mazdaznan into French. Through its emphasis upon the link between spiritual evolution and physical exercises, Mazdaznan may well have played the role of a precursor to yoga.[9]

Around the same time, the first followers of the Baha'i Faith became active in Switzerland; they were, however, to remain a very small group until after the Second World War. As early as 1920, Hazrat Inayat Khan (1882-1927) was able to find some followers in Geneva, where he established the international head-quarters of the Sufi Movement (1923). The famous French author, Romain Rolland (1866-1944), also had his residence on the shores of the Geneva lake, and there he wrote the biographies of Ramakrishna and Vivekananda for Western readers; thus he paved the way for the work of another French citizen living in Switzerland, Jean Herbert (1897-1980), who, in the 1930s, began to translate the teachings of several contemporary Hindu spiritual masters. In the perspective of Rolland and Herbert, the purpose was not to convert Westerners to the Hindu religion, but rather to open their eyes towards another spiritual world. However, there is no doubt that their work prepared the grounds for those souls who would be ready to take one step further towards the East. At a time when still very few Eastern religious movements had established a presence in Switzerland, the role played by books should not be underestimated. Just before the Second World War, one can notice the first signs of activity of the Radha Soami movement (through the work of an homeopathic physician living in Geneva, Pierre Schmidt (d.1987), and of followers of Meher Baba.

After having spent several years in Hungary, the Indian yoga teacher Selvarajan Yesudian, settled in Switzerland in 1948.[10] He founded the first yoga schools in Switzerland and published several books which clearly contain certain aspects of a spiritual background although the books also are mixed with attempts to make yoga as acceptable as possible to the Christians of the West.[11] From 1951 a periodical with the title *Synthèse universelle* was published in Geneva (subtitle: 'Monthly for the spiritual progress of mankind'). Among the contributors were theosophists as well as followers of Ramakrishna or Yogananda. In 1954 the periodical became the official organ of the European branch of Swami Sivananda's Divine Life Society, though it continued to publish information about other movements or even messages supposedly coming from extraterrestrial entities. This periodical bears witness to the existence and activity of a cultic milieu in Switzerland already at that time.

From 1960 to 1990 Switzerland then experienced the arrival of most of the well-known Eastern movements which are also active in the other European countries. To mention just a few:

Between *1950* and *1969*: the Self-Realization Fellowship (Yogananda), the Ramakrishna Mission, Subud, the Divine Light Zentrum (Swami Omkarananda, follower of Sivananda), and Transcendental Meditation established local groups in Switzerland.

Between *1970* and *1979*: ISKCON, Ananda Marga, Sri Chinmoy Centres, Siddha Yoga, Sawan Kirpal Ruhani Mission, Shri Ram Chandra Mission, Unification Church, Mahikari.

Between *1980* and *1989*: Brahma Kumaris, Sahaja Yoga, followers of Mata Amritanandamayi...

Several more could be added to this list, but it will be sufficient to observe that compared with countries like the United States or Great Britain, the context was different: the presence of immigrants from the mother countries of these religious groups has played very little role in the establishment of such movements in Switzerland. The devotees of Sathya Sai Baba are among the very few Eastern movements where Western followers interact with a significant number of devotees from the Indian subcontinent. When they celebrate major Hindu festivals, the Krishna devotees, too, welcome quite a large number of Hindu visitors (including the Indian ambassador himself), and, in 1991 they formed an association especially designed for Tamils residing in Switzerland (following the influx of several thousand Tamil asylum seekers from Sri Lanka). But these two movements are more the exception than the rule.

There had already been some signs of a Buddhist activity in Switzerland during the first half of the twentieth century, but nothing stable before the end of the Second World War. A turning point was the foundation of a 'Buddhistische Gemeinschaft' in Zurich in 1942. In 1948 it launched a periodical entitled *Die Einsicht. Schweizerische Zeitschrift für Buddhismus*, which proved to be quite helpful for Buddhists in post-war Germany, too; the orientation was clearly Theravada. Later, the arrival of a Tibetan community in exile, which led to the foundation of a Tibetan monastery in Rikon, most certainly contributed to the development of an interest towards Tibetan Buddhism. In 1967 in Geneva, the modest activity of the Soka Gakkai was launched by meetings of a group of Japanese members.

Naturally, alternative religiosity is by no means restricted to the East. Upon the foundation of the 'Société vaudoise d'études psychiques' (created in 1927 in Lausanne), Dr Edouard Bertholet (1883-1965) launched *c.* 1933 a Rosicrucian Order in cooperation with a German citizen, August Reichel (1898-1962). During the 50s, the Rosicrucian Order AMORC as well as the Lectorium Rosicrucianum developed their activities in Switzerland. Previously though, in the 40s, the Universal White Brotherhood (Omraam Mikhaël Aïvanhov) and the I AM Activity had gained a foothold.

Current situation

During our research, we have been able to gather detailed information about the geographical distribution (local groups) of 41 representative movements (Eastern movements, occult groups, UFO believers, etc.). Complete tables can be found in our book.[12] Among these 41 movements, there are 32 with a local branch in the canton of Zurich, and 29 in the canton of Geneva. Given the fact that Zurich is the most heavily populated city and canton, there is nothing surprising about the first figure. The Geneva figure, on the other hand, is more surprising since the canton only has one-third of that of the Zurich canton population, still it nearly reaches the same amount of movements as Zurich. This 'anomaly' is worth a closer look.

In their article 'Europe's Receptivity to Cults and Sects',[13] the American sociologists Stark and Bainbridge explain Switzerland as a 'deviant case' when compared to the statistical data gathered about other countries. At the same time, Switzerland is a country where the conventional Catholic and Protestant Churches are still vigorous and 'scores high on all cult measures'. But, according to the two sociologists, the national rate is actually greatly inflated by the statistical data of Geneva: they know of no other city in the world where the rate of sects and cults would be so high when compared to the total population.

We are very reluctant to go as far as Bainbridge and Stark, but we have to admit that our own findings confirm that same high rate of new religious movements in Geneva (it should, however, be added here that the data which we have been able to gather do not allow us, for all groups, to know the number of followers they have in each canton: we have accurate statistical data about the number of groups in each canton, but only for part of these groups we have data about the number of local members). However, according to the missionaries of several movements, Geneva is not a city where their work is always easy. For instance, although they initially settled in Geneva, the Krishna devotees, due to poor results, decided after a few years to close the centre which they had established there, and they have since been recruiting mainly in the German-speaking part of the country. The Church of Scientology has never been able to grow as much in Geneva as it would have wished.

Nevertheless, even if their number of followers remains modest there, many movements are at least able to establish a small presence in Geneva. How can we account for that fact? One must understand that Geneva is an atypical Swiss city, also in other respects, and although its population is not very large when compared to major European and North American cities, Geneva is an important international centre. It is our opinion that this characteristic would explain, at least partly, the unusual situation as to new religious movements in Geneva. In Geneva, there is an unusually large international community in which English is a widespread language (many people who spend years working in international organizations in Geneva can avoid the trouble of having to learn French). The many international connections of Geneva and the presence of a large number of international organizations make it a very attractive place for new religious movements to gain a foothold. Already in 1920, Sufi Master Inayat Khan considered Geneva and Switzerland a good springboard.[14]

The fact that one should be cautious about drawing conclusions from the Geneva data is reinforced by the case of the canton of Tessin, which, while being very different from the canton of Geneva, has a rate not very much below Geneva's. And, again, one may ask whether there is a link between this unexpected result and the presence of many people from outside? At the beginning of the twentieth century, the Monte Verità had already attracted many utopians and occultists to this area. But very few among these 'spiritual seekers' were Swiss, and nearly none were local people... Once again, such results show that statistical data, no matter how interesting they may be, must be treated carefully and that non-statistical factors should be used as well.

Although Switzerland plays host to many new religious movements, it does not seem to be a very productive country in this respect: except for some *Neuoffenbarungen* and the FIGU (Freie Interessengemeinschaft für Grenz- und Geisteswissenschaften und Ufologiestudien), a group founded by Eduard ('Billy') Meier, few movements have exclusively Swiss roots. One might say that today's religious pluralism in Switzerland to a very large extent, is the result of importations.

The constant growth in the supply in the religious market is obvious. However, apart from a few exceptions (most of all the Anthroposophic Society, which has its world headquarters in Switzerland and gathers between 4,000 and 5,000 members, not to mention the impact of some initiatives like the Steiner schools), the addition of the members of all the movements would give a rather limited total number — and one should not forget that the level of involvement may vary a lot from one movement to another. Rather than being the development of some individual group, it is the simultaneous activity of a growing number of small groups which create an interesting phenomenon. Besides Anthroposophy, only scientologists and baha'is have been able to cross the threshold of 1,000 followers in Switzerland.[15] Unless very unexpected circumstances intervene, it seems highly unlikely that one of these movements could suddenly experience a lightning growth — and even more so since there are always more groups trying to find their niche in the 'market'! For this reason, rather than to focus on this or that movement coming temporarily into the limelight, it seems more appropriate to take the global phenomenon of the cultic milieu as the main objective for future research and analysis. Most of the movements are manifestations of the global alternative religiosity — the most visible manifestation, no doubt, but not necessarily the most important factor contributing to the transformation of the religious landscape in the long run.

New religious movements and the Swiss society

The development of religious pluralism inevitably walks hand in hand with tensions and conflicts. There is nothing new about this: when the Salvation Army reached Switzerland in the nineteenth century, it did not happen without a lot of controversy and fierce reactions.[16] In the same way, around 1920, the establishment of the world centre of the Anthroposophic Society in Dornach gave rise to quite a turmoil in the region.[17] But most of the movements we are dealing with here remain ignored by the general public[18] and they enjoy a rather peaceful existence in obscurity.

In some cases, however, tensions arise and become public affair. Some are instances of localized conflicts. One is the case of the Divine Light Zentrum (DLZ), founded in Winterthur in 1966 under the spiritual leadership of Swami Omkarananda (born 1940). In 1968 and onwards, the movement experienced increasingly conflicts in its interaction with its neighbours and local authorities. The tensions led to court cases, political interventions, and even several crimes committed by DLZ members, including a bomb attack against the private house of the police director (October 1975). In 1979, several members were sentenced to jail, including Swami Omkarananda himself (who was expelled from Switzerland after his release on parole in 1985).

Given the origins of the DLZ, one might be inclined to believe that conflict may have something to do with the degree of 'exoticism' of the group. But this is not really the case: many Eastern movements do not experience difficulties, whereas one of the most spectacular conflicts of the past decade involved a group called 'Michaelsvereinigung', which has its centre in the village of Dozwil (Thurgau). The movement was founded in the 1960s by a gardener, Paul Kuhn (born 1920). Although he himself had been raised as a Protestant, he draws followers to a kind of traditional-looking Catholic worship, mixed with revelations from above in the typical style of the *Neuoffenbarungen* and teachings like reincarnation. In 1988 (Spring), a sensationalist newspaper gave large coverage to apocalyptic prophecies, then unwisely spread among the local population by the Michaelsvereinigung; the paper was able to create such a hysteria that hooligan-like crowds gathered in the village and caused a lot of damage. In short, the newspaper had predicted so strongly that this would generate riot-like events in Dozwil, that it thereby actually created them! (Most of the other newspapers strongly condemned this unethical journalistic behaviour.)

The above-mentioned example clearly shows that movements, which to a wide degree belong to our cultural area, can experience very strong reactions. But the extent of the DLZ cases as well as the 'Michaelsvereinigung' is small. First, they are not widespread geographically, and, secondly, they are (at least in part) a consequence of the massive settlement of a group in a local community. On the other hand, there are also movements which do not encounter a localized opposition, but which give rise to widespread reactions: one such case is the Church of Scientology, which has critics in all the areas in the country where it has branches, in a way very similar to other places in the world where the movement is active. Naturally, Scientology is not the only controversial new religious movement, but it is no doubt the most frequently criticized one in Switzerland. Part of the explanation could be that it gets in touch with a lot more people than other controversial movements, since it is very active in propagating its practices, and, at first hand, does not offer a philosophical message, but a method claiming to develop the individual's potential.

The development of new religious movements has not passed unnoticed by both the representatives of the conventional Churches as well as other public institutions. Quite early, some churchmen became aware of the phenomenon of new religious movements, and especially of the import of Eastern messages into the West. Among these were the Roman Catholic priest and philosopher Gebhard Frei (1905-67), who also showed a great interest in parapsychology,[19] and — most of all — the Reformed theologian Fritz Blanke[20] who, in the 50s, published three successive editions of a guidebook about contemporary religious movements, in which several pages were devoted to non-Christian religious movements.[21] The Reformed minister, Rev. Oswald Eggenberger, has continued the efforts of Blanke, and, in 1963, founded the 'Evangelische Orientierungsstelle' in Zurich. For many years, Eggenberger published a quarterly bulletin about sects and new religious movements. Since 1993 the bulletin has been edited by the Ecumenical Study Group on New Religious Movements.

The Ecumenical Study Group on New Religious Movements is under the supervision of both the Swiss Roman Catholic Bishops Conference and the Federation of Protestant Churches of Switzerland; it has been active since 1980 (upon the basis of a Roman Catholic study group launched in 1979). Switzerland was probably the first country where the Roman Catholic Church and the Protestant Church from the beginning decided to create an interconfessional organ to answer the challenge of new religions.

On the other hand, a regional information and advice centre, the 'Beratungsstelle für Sektenfragen', had been created in Luzern in 1980 under the tutelage of the local Roman Catholic Church. Vicar Reiner Krieger and theologian Hugo Sidler were put in charge of the centre. For various reasons the activity of the centre led to tensions within the Church, which meant that it was closed at the end of 1988. However, in cooperation with the Ecumenical Study Group, a new centre was later opened under a new leadership (a Reformed minister) in an ecumenical perspective (Roman Catholic/Reformed).

At local and cantonal political levels one has witnessed isolated statements regarding new religious movements, usually in connection with specific cases. At federal level the topic of new religious movements has never been a major issue, and it has never led to big debates in the Parliament. In 1987, however, the Section for Consular Protection of the Swiss Ministry for Foreign Affairs issued a warning aimed particularly at young Swiss people travelling to the United States to stay there for some time to learn English. This warning followed several complaints by Swiss families who had had a son or a daughter converted to the Unification Church while staying in California. In March 1987 in order to draw their attention towards the occurence of such problems, the Section for Consular Protection sent a letter to some thirty agencies which were providing young people with opportunities for language stays. The interpretation of the phenomenon described in the letter tended towards an 'anti-cult' argumentation; several controversial new religious movements complained about this approach. Later, a well-known member of Parliament from the canton of Geneva, Gilles Petitpierre, asked the federal government to give its opinion regarding the 'recruitment into sects and breach of personal freedom'. In its answer of March 1989 (which refers to the above-mentioned letter from the Section for Consular Protection), the Federal Government commented, among other things:

(...) there are many possibilities for legal and State intervention against abuses committed by organizations claiming to be religious. However, one should take into account the limited reach of measures through the law and the State. No monitoring, no supervision, even of an intensive nature, will be able to prevent some tragic deviations. In addition, human and relational emotions go very often beyond what can be circumscribed by legal norms. Besides, it is essential to know to which extent the commitment, the limitations of freedom and the patrimonial sacrifices accepted by an individual in favour of a sect are or are not the result of that person's free will (...) In addition to State measures, mainly private initiatives or initiatives sponsored by the national Churches, this area is a good field for action. Nevertheless, the crucial element for receptivity or resistence of an individual faced with entreaties from new religious movements lies first of all with the principles acquired by the individual in his family, school and religious environment, i.e. principles which have left their mark on the development of the individuality.

Regarding the 'private initiatives' mentioned in the document from the Federal Government, Switzerland has experienced the development of some anti-cult groups created by people anxious about the development of new religious movements. Anti-cult groups were born in Switzerland somewhat later than in France or in Germany. In the French-speaking part of Switzerland, the 'Association pour la défense de la famille et de l'individu — Suisse' (ADFIS), whose name indicates a parentage with a similar association in France, was founded by a Reformed deacon (with evangelical leanings), Paul Ranc, who had written a booklet about the controversial evangelist Jean-Michel Cravanzola.[22] Created in 1983, the association went through more or less active periods, due to serious health problems experienced by its founder. In November 1988 it was reorganized and relaunched. Shortly afterwards, however, a severe crisis followed, when, in January 1989 it was discovered that the ADFIS secretary was actually an active member of Sahaja Yoga! The ADFIS very nearly disintegrated, but was, however, able to survive. It saw a new leadership and merged with a small group named 'Centre Info-Sectes', launched by a former scientologist. In 1993 for some time, it adopted the name 'Info-Sectes'; yet in 1994 after another change in the presidency, it seems to have returned to a name similar to the original one ('Association suisse pour la défense de la famille et de l'individu'). In addition, in the canton of Vaud, there is a 'Bureau d'aide et d'information sur les mouvements religieux' (BAIMR), founded by former members of the ADFIS, following the 1989 crisis. Under the leadership of Françoise Elsig, the BAIMR tries to follow a line somewhat similar to that of INFORM in Great Britain.

Finally, in 1994, François Lavergnat launched a new anti-cult group, the 'Groupement de protection de la famille et de l'individu' (GPFI), which is quite active in the area of Geneva.

Only as late as 1987, in the German-speaking part of Switzerland, an anti-cult group emerged. The 'Schweizerische Arbeitsgemeinschaft gegen destruktive Kulte' (SADK) had as its main source the parents of young Swiss people who, while in the United States, had converted to the Unification Church. Later, relatives of converts to other new religious movements joined the SADK, too. The SADK also has an Italian-speaking branch in Tessin. The SADK wasted no time as they took a more decisive line of action than the ADFIS did; for instance it commissioned a legal expert's interesting report about existing possibilities to counter 'cults'.[23] In contrast to ADFIS (and still more to BAIMR), several leading members of the SADK have never made it a secret that they sympathize with the practice of deprogramming. In November 1988 they even invited the well-known British deprogrammer Martin Faiers, to a press conference. A family in Tessin, linked to the SADK, was in 1989 the source of the highly publicized case of a failed attempt to 'deprogramme' a Krishna devotee.[24] In addition, in Zurich in 1991, 'Infosekta', an information centre, was founded and financially supported by both the local Churches and the local and cantonal authorities. This led to protests from Scientologists and Moonies. At the end of 1992, however, 'Infosekta' had to somewhat reduce its activities due to financial difficulties, because some of the initial subventions had not been renewed.

The tragedy of the Solar Temple (53 dead in Québec and Switzerland in October 1994 and 16 more in France in December 1995) struck the Swiss public opinion. The growing controversies around Scientology in Germany and other countries are frequently mentioned in the Swiss media too. It can be expected that more attention will be given to the topic in the years to come. A first sign has been the publication, in February 1997, of a 300 page long expert's report about the legal possibilities of prevention in the field of sects, written upon request of a member of the cantonal government of Geneva. It remains however to be seen if, and how, some of the 40 suggestions made in the report will be implemented.

Conclusion

At the junction of three linguistic areas of Europe, Switzerland, to a rather large extent, is under the cultural influences from its neighbouring countries. For this reason, it comes as no surprise that we experience a religious panorama which seems to reflect quite adequately the current situation on the European continent. In Switzerland, as elsewhere, behind the new religious movements, a diffuse alternative religiosity is gaining ground, as illustrated by esoteric fairs or bookshops. Research about new religious movements acquires its full meaning only when put into a wider perspective: new religious movements then begin to appear as likely forerunners of a situation of new religious pluralism where the individualization of religious 'options' tends to become characteristic. But this individualization brings in itself the limits to the potential success of each individual group. For this reason, at this point, it seems practically impossible to determine what the future will be for most of the movements (and which ones will be able to survive in the long run). However, there is no doubt that we will continue to see, year after year, new movements reaching the Swiss religious market, although the potential for each of them will probably remain modest.

Notes

1. The author of this paper had investigated this movement in Switzerland in the 80s, at a time when it was still ignored; see J.-F. Mayer, 'Des templiers pour l'Ere du Verseau: les Clubs Archédia (1984-1991) et l'Ordre International Chevaleresque Tradition Solaire', in *Mouvements religieux*, No. 153, January 1993, pp. 2-10. For a summary about the case, see J.-F. Mayer, *Les Mythes du Temple Solaire*, Geneva: Georg, 1996.

2. J.-F. Mayer, *Les nouvelle voies spirituelles. Enquête sur la religiosité parallèle en Suisse*, Lausanne: L'Age d'Homme, 1993.

3. Louis Carlen, 'Le statut juridique des Eglises en Suisse', in *Les Eglises et le Fédéralisme*, Fribourg: Institut du Fédéralisme/Editions Universitaires, 1990, pp. 5-14 (p. 10). For a recent overview, see Adrian Loretan, *Rapports Eglise-Etat en mutation*, Fribourg: Editions Universitaires, 1997.

4. Augustin Macheret, 'Les Eglises de l'Etat: séparables ou inséparables', in ibid., pp. 15-31 (p. 22).

5.   See D.D. Home, *Les Lumières et les Ombres du Spiritualisme*, Paris 1883, pp. 102-10.

6.   Kurt Hutten, *Seher — Grübler —Enthusiasten. Das Buch der traditionellen Sekten und religiösen Sonderbewegungen* (13th ed.), Stuttgart: Quell Verlag, 1984, pp. 747-54.

7.   Eugène Lévy, *Madame Annie Besant et la crise de la Société théosophique*, Paris 1913, p. 36.

8.   For instance, one could mention here Anna Kamensky (1867-1952), a Russian theosophist in exile, who cared for the survival of the Russian Section of the Theosophical Society abroad, and who taught the science of religion at the University of Geneva (see Victor B. Fedjuschin, *Russlands Sehnsucht nach Spiritualität. Theosophie, Anthroposophie und die Russen*, Schaffhausen: Novalis Verlag, 1988. pp. 80-84).

9.   Olivier Moulin and Thierry Wetterwald, *Les marchands de bien-être. Exploration du milieu genevois des diffuseurs de techniques de modification de l'état de conscience* (University of Geneva, Department of Sociology, 1986), p. 61.

10. See S. Yesudian, *Confiance en soi par le yoga*, Lausanne: Editions du Signal, 1983 (especially chapter 1).

11. See S. Yesudian and Elisabeth Haich, *Yoga Uniting East and West*, London: Allen & Unwin, 1956.

12. J.-F. Mayer, *Les nouvelles voies spirituelles*, p. 275.

13. Rodney Stark and William Sims Bainbridge, *The Future of Religion*, Berkeley: University of California Press, 1985, pp. 475-505 (especially pp. 498-502). Recently, Stark has answered some critics about the article and added new precisions (R. Stark, 'Europe's Receptivity to New Religious Movements: Round Two', *Journal for the Scientific Study of Religion*, 32:4, Dec. 1993, pp. 389-97); we do not think that all the problems which were raised are solved through that answer, but this is not the place for further discussion — anyway, the development of such debates is much welcome in order to stimulate comparative approaches and to discuss some common assumptions.

14. Elisabeth de Jong-Keesing, *Inayat Khan. A Biography*, The Hague: East-West Publications Fonds , 1974, pp. 168 and 173.

15. Transcendental Meditation actually claims 12,000 initiates, but this is the cumulative number of all those who have been initiated since the beginning of the movement in Switzerland in the 1960s, including those who have died, those who have become members of other movements, and those who long ago lost any interest in TM; this means that a huge part of these 12,000 initiates are not likely to be in touch with TM as an organization anymore.

16. See J.-F. Mayer, *Une honteuse exploitation des esprits et des porte-monnaie?*, Fribourg: Les Trois Nornes, 1985.

17. This is documented in our book *Les nouvelles voies spirituelles*, pp. 307-11.

18. For instance, insofar as we are aware, the Swiss media had never published a critical article about the now (in)famous Solar Temple.

19. See Theo Locher, *Parapsychologie in der Schweiz gestern und heute*, Biel: Schweizerische Vereinigung für Parapsychologie, 1986, pp. 94-99.

20. See Fritz Blanke, 'Asiatische religiöse Strümungen in Europa', in *Die Einheit der Kirche und die Sekten*, Zollikon: Evangelischer Verlag, 1959.

21. Fritz Blanke, *Kirchen und Sekten. Führer durch die religiöse Gruppen der Gegenwart* (3rd ed.), Zürich/Stuttgart: Zwingli Verlag, 1959. Oswald Eggenberger has continued that line with a well-documented and useful handbook: *Die Kirchen, Sondergruppen und religiösen Vereinigungen* (6th ed.), Zürich: Theologischer Verlag, 1994.

22. Paul Ranc, *Et si ce n'était pas vrai? Une évaluation de la doctrine de Jean-Michel Cravanzola*, Lausanne: Editions du Rocher, 1979. Subsequently, Ranc published a much longer book about Rosicrucianism as well as critical books about New Age, Free-Masonry and (in 1993) Scientology.

23. *Sekten im rechtsfreien Raum?*, Zürich: Presdok, 1990.

24. For a detailed report about this case, see J.-F. Mayer, *Confessions d'un chasseur de sectes*, Paris: Editions du Cerf, 1990 (chapter 8).

CHAPTER 7

New Religious Movements in the Republic of Ireland

Mike Garde

Introduction

Unlike most of Europe, Ireland was not invaded by the Romans. Thus, from an early time the island has always been somewhat outside of the mainstream of European life. Once Ireland became Christian, the Church assimilated elements of indigenous Irish culture. In this regard, it is notable that the development of Christianity did not include the banning of paganism, as in central Europe. Christianity was built on the existing pagan belief, which resulted in a sort of peaceful coexistence.

Consequently, Ireland had an independent Celtic Christian tradition until the invasion of the Anglo-Normans at the end of the twelfth century. The arrival of Christians from the continent brought the medieval practices of Europe onto the island. Centuries later, while the Reformation was experienced as a liberating movement in many parts of Europe, in Ireland Protestantism was associated with English colonial rule. In the seventeenth century, a policy of Protestant church planting in the north, east and southeast parts of the country was undertaken, but only succeeded in the north. This tended to lead to the identification of Catholicism with Irish nationalism from the nineteenth century. Up until this century, when Ireland was divided in 1922, the Christian faith was the predominant world view of the people. Due to lack of contact, Roman Catholics and Protestants tended to see each other as 'different religions'. At the end of the last century Eastern thought was made popular by Theosophy, founded by Madame Blavatsky and spread by others. In Ireland it had exponents like the famous Nobel prize-winning poet W.B. Yeats. However, Ireland remained quite cut off and insular until its membership of the European Community in 1972.

The conflict in Northern Ireland, and the advent of a national television service in the 1960s have all led to a questioning of the Christian consensus in recent years. Even though the churches are experiencing decline, attendance is still among the highest in the world (see chart below), and this makes the advent of new religious movements difficult, as they tend to find their largest audience where traditional Christianity is weakest.

European Values Survey 1990 — Confidence in Church

('a great deal' + 'quite a lot', 1990, in %)

	All Ages	18-24 years	Difference
Northern Ireland	80	60	-20
Ireland	72	53	-19
Italy	60	55	-5
Portugal	63	47	-16
Spain	49	33	-16
Belgium	51	34	-17
France	49	34	-15
Great Britain	45	31	-14
Germany	38	23	-15
The Netherlands	32	32	–
European (average)	51	38	-13

Most new religious movements came to Ireland from Britain or the USA when young people returned home after working or studying abroad.

However, there is generally little interest in the academic community concerning the phenomenon of new religious movements, and the media tend to describe any non-Catholic group as a 'cult'. This results in fear when young people experiment with NRMs. This was highlighted in Ireland in November 1978 after the Jonestown massacre in Guyana and in 1993 with the Waco, Texas tragedy. In Ireland the Mary Canning story is quite interesting and revealing. A teacher, who joined the Unification Church in California, came back proclaiming her new faith. Two weeks later she was deprogrammed and subsequently appeared before Government authorities to say she was brainwashed. Generally the media tend to merely repeat old news, and rarely investigate the movements in depth or by first-hand research. They rely on ex-members or anti-cult views to form judgments about the movements.

The group which is most feared is called the 'born again' movement. These are mainly American-style evangelicals who do not regard the Catholic Church as a Christian church. They offer an immediate sense of salvation against the church's sacramental emphasis. They are seen as cults, as opposed to the Protestant Church of Ireland (Anglican), Presbyterian, Methodist and Quakers, who are recognised as 'separated Christians' since the Second Vatican Council.

One of the latest arrivals here is the Dublin Church of Christ, a branch of the Boston Church of Christ. It has about 50 members. Also, the 'Family', formerly COG, came back to Ireland but now, other than visiting teams, is no longer resident here. Other movements which have been here for much longer are The Church of the Latter Day Saints (Mormons), and the Jehovah's Witnesses. The former have been in Ireland since the 1840s. The Mormons offer a sense of mystery, whereas the Jehovah's Witnesses reduce the mysterious, e.g. the Trinity to Jehovah. They have over 800 full-time workers and can be found all over the country.

In recent years one of the groups that have been most visible has been the Unification Church. Even though it has a very small membership, it has nearly had to go undergound because of adverse reaction in the media.

ISKCON (Hare Krishna) had a higher profile but through internal divisions are now reduced in influence. The School of Philosophy and Economic Science has been in Ireland for 25 years and has a large number of centres around the country, with over 2,000 participants in its programmes. Scientology has had a mission in Dublin since 1987, and in January 1997 it became an organization here, and plans a mission in every county in Ireland. It received negative publicity in February 1995 when it was the subject of a major Irish TV programme called 'The Late Late Show' featuring the Dialogue Centre and members of Scientology in open debate.

Another movement which is hard to categorise is the New Age Movement, which in Ireland tends to connect with a neo-pagan undercurrent which has existed since ancient days. It connects especially with feminists who feel lost in a male clerical church. It has connections with creation-based spirituality of Matthew Fox as well as Celtic spirituality with its return to pre-Christian roots.

Other groups here are the New Acropolis, the EMIN Foundation, the Gnostic Movement, I AM (now called Outlook), the Inner Peace Movement, Eckankar, and Transcendental Meditation (TM) which has been in Ireland for some years.

All these movements can be found throughout Ireland, but the main concentration is in the Dublin area.

Cults vs. New Religious Movements

The term 'cult', which might be defined as a group with an 'open' belief system, has now come to mean exactly the opposite. It is now taken to be a closed group with an authoritarian leader and a rigid set of doctrines. The people in it are regarded as brainwashed, or at least under mind control. In fact it does not matter what beliefs they have, they are all suspected of being subject to mind control. The advantage of the term 'religious movement' is that it allows for an examination of the various movements without shutting down discussion from the start, as is the case with the term 'cult'.

The term 'religious movement' also allows one to affix the adjectives 'new' or 'old' wherever appropriate. For example, the Mormons, whose organization is more than 100 years old, can be spoken of as an 'older' religious movement, whereas Scientology is definitely a new religious movement.

Numbers

(a) *Professionals*. There are no statistics, nor is there a system of accreditation by the Department of Health, so anyone can put up a sign offering healing or counselling. There is an increasing number of centres offering counselling etc. Nationally I would estimate that there are over 1,000 NRM professionals.

(b) *Members in Movements*. The evangelical groups have on the average about 40-50 members. Groups like the Unification Church, which gets massive media attention, have an extremely small membership. Many of their local members are serving abroad, leaving a small skeleton staff behind. However, Christian deviations like the Jehovah's Witnesses and the Mormons are currently seeing rapid growth.

Moreover, there is some degree of overlap. New Age groups are less membership-oriented and people could be members of some 'centre' and involved with the Catholic Church at the same time.

(c) *Influence of New Religious Movements*. Certainly many of the beliefs of the NRMs are finding a resonance in public life which is much wider than the membership of the NRMs themselves. Scientology's belief in former lives and ISKCON's teaching of reincarnation is widely accepted in Ireland as in Europe generally. People seem to hold to contradictory beliefs simultaneously and without much reflection, ie. resurrection and reincarnation.

There is also no awareness of the contradiction between Catholic faith and the use of tarot cards, fortune-telling, astrology and palmistry. Again, they co-exist happily, as there has always been a tolerance of these kinds of things within the Catholic Church in Ireland.

Receptivity of Church and State to New Religious Movements

According to Article 44 of the Irish Constitution (44.1.1) the state acknowledges that the homage of public worship is due to Almighty God. It shall hold His name in reverence, and shall respect and honour religion. The following sections were deleted in a 1972 referendum:

The State recognises the special position of the Holy Catholic Apostolic and Roman Church as the Guardian of the Faith professed by the great majority of the citizens. (44.1.2)

The State also recognises the Church of Ireland, the Presbyterian Church in Ireland, the Methodist Church in Ireland, the Religious Society of Friends in Ireland, as well as the Jewish congregations and other religious denominations existing in Ireland at the date of the coming into operation of this Constitution. (44.1.3)

Freedom of conscience and the free profession and practice of religion are, subject to public order and morality, guaranteed to every citizen. (44.2.1)

The State guarantees not to endow any religion. (44.2.2)

The State shall not impose any disabilities or make any discrimination on the grounds of religious profession, belief or status. (44.2.3)

The Irish State effectively guarantees the separation of church and state and provides a mandate for the exercise of the NRMs' faith. This separation is understood in proportional terms, i.e. even though the state promises not to endow any religion, it still supports denominational schooling, and in fact tends to give a higher proportion to Protestant schools and hospitals than their numbers warrant.

Groups concerned with NRMs

In the early eighties there was a branch of the American Family Foundation established in Ireland called 'The Irish Family Foundation'. They no longer exist, but there are two anti-cult organizations with an evangelical orientation. There are also:

(a) *Irish Church Missions Cult Department*
This is an English Anglican mission organization whose primary goal is the conversion of Catholics, but more recently they have taken up the anti-cult activity under Noel Deane, a former Catholic who flirted briefly with the Unification Church. The approach centres on an evangelical apologetic and refutation of the cults. They service the tabloid newspapers with cult stories.
Address:
ICM Cult Department
Bachelor's Walk
Dublin 1
Tel. 353-1-8722669
Fax 353-1-8730829

(b) Less active in media or direct work with NRMs, but more active in seminars is the *Cult Awareness Centre* headed by Mick Toolan. They are agents for the Reachout Trust in the UK. They are based in a Baptist church.
Address:
28a Pearse Street
Dublin 2
Tel. 353-1-8339650

(c) *The Dialogue Centre* is modelled on the centre of the same name in Aarhus, Denmark, and provides information on the NRMs in Ireland. It researches their teachings and enters into dialogue with its members. They also help families and try to help members leave groups through discussion and information, providing a counselling service for people affected, whether family or members. In the Irish context the Dialogue Centre is also ecumenically established in that it represents the Church of Ireland (Anglican), Methodist, Presbyterian and Roman Catholic churches. Address:

7/8 Lower Abbey Street
Dublin 1
Tel. 353-1-8309384; 353-1-8788177
Fax. 353-1-8744913

Kidnapping/Deprogramming

If you believe that your son or daughter has been brainwashed or is under the influence of a mind control cult, you would tend to consider deprogramming or kidnapping as a means to remedy the situation. On the other hand, if you believe the person has undergone a religious conversion, that kind of activity would be regarded as criminal. There have been examples of people using deprogramming methods with no sense of shame; over ten years ago a member of the Irish governemnt colluded in such an activity. However, none of these cases have come to court so we cannot really evaluate what judgment might be rendered on these activities.

Conclusion

The influence of NRMs is that of a growing minority. As Ireland becomes more pluralistic, it is not becoming secular but more multi-layered in its religious expression.

Ireland is generally an insular society and although there is a very international awareness beyond our borders, i.e. pro-European integration, support for liberation in Africa, concern for famine relief etc., there is a tendency to be quite resistant to change in Ireland. Change is being forced upon the churches and the State and the NRM scene is part of these changes.

CHAPTER 8

New Religious Movements in Britain

Eileen Barker

Introduction

Throughout her history, from pagan times to the present, new religious movements (NRMs) have been brought to, or created on, the soil of the United Kingdom. For the past millennium and longer, the NRMs have been almost entirely of the Judaeo Christian tradition. There have, however, been the exceptions that proved the rule: in Victorian times, there was considerable interest in the paranormal — spiritualism, Mesmerism, occultism and astrology, and there was a limited popularisation of Eastern thought by Madame Blavatsky, reinforced by the British occultist Annie Besant (1847-1933) who 'discovered' the young Krishna-murti and was President of the Theosophical Society from 1907 until her death. Alice Bailey, who was born in Victorian Manchester in 1880, P.D. Ouspensky, who moved to London at the outbreak of the Russian Revolution, and other eccentrics of the period may well have been the heralds of things to come. Certainly, by the middle of the twentieth century, there were those (mainly members of middle-class, literary circles) in English society who were aware of, or even embraced, the thought of Steiner, Gurdjieff, Ramakrishna, and the two contemporary exponents of magic: Aleister Crowley (1875-1947) and Gerald Gardner (1884-1960), both of whom were British. But the general public was for the most part unaware of, and unconcerned about, 'foreign', 'bizarre' and/or 'pagan' beliefs and practices.

During the 1950s, however, there emerged in Britain a youth culture — or, rather, a number of youth cultures within both the working and the middle classes.[1] The working-class culture was genuinely innovative and indigenous to Britain, with Teds, Mods, Rockers, Punks and other groups expressing their identity through dress and music, rather than through religion. Indeed, very few

NRMs have attracted a sizeable working-class membership; the Rastafarian appeal to unemployed black youth, and the Jesus Army's appeal to inner-city 'down-and-outs' are among the few exceptions.

Paths of exploration for middle-class youth, disproportionately investigated by members of the student population, roughly paralleled those in North America and other parts of Western Europe. They shifted from political attempts to change the structure of society to the hippie rejection of all structures; then they turned to embrace religious and spiritual roads to salvation — either in the next world or, increasingly, in this; and then to seek 'the God within' in the attempt to realise the 'true self'.[2] During the 1960s and the first half of the 1970s, the mass media in Britain paid relatively little attention to the new movements, apart from reporting particular incidents such as when, in 1968, the British Government imposed restrictions on foreigners entering the UK to study, or work for, Scientology (see below), and a limited flurry of excitement in 1973 when it was revealed that some British students had been invited to New York by the Unification Church.

Then, as elsewhere, the visibility of the movements grew, culminating in an explosion of media coverage in November 1978 when the Jonestown suicides and murders in Guyana forcibly brought into public view the potential danger of the 'cults', whom the media and general public tended, and still tend, indiscriminately to lump together as a single, undesirable entity. A further event that had extensive coverage in Britain was the *Daily Mail* case in the early 1980s, when the Unification Church lost a libel suit against the tabloid for saying that it brainwashed its members and broke up families (see below).[3]

But although NRMs have received an unfavourable press and there have been some severe attacks made on them in public by anti-cult groups and some clergy and Members of Parliament, their rights have, by and large, been protected so long as they have stayed within the law. No *British* citizen has been forbidden to practice the religion of his or her choice. The only instances in which adults have been prevented from practicing their religion are when parents, who have no legal rights over adult children, have either locked up their sons or daughters themselves, or paid someone else to attempt a forcible 'deprogramming'.[4] As the practice is illegal, it is not easy to know exact numbers, but there have certainly been at least forty, and possibly as many as one hundred such attempts by British parents; and there have been a number of occasions when a British deprogramming has been discussed in the media with approval — or actually shown on television.[5]

While the greatest visibility of the movements was around the late 1970s and early 1980s, when special attention was paid to the Unification Church and the Church of Scientology, the media have continued, and still continue, to run stories on any religious beliefs or practices that deviate from the mainstream traditions. Those movements whose existence is relatively well-known to the British public include ISKCON, *est* (now known as the Forum), the Jesus Army, the Rajneeshees, Transcendental Meditation and the New Age. During the early 1990s, the press have been concentrating on a number of stories about the London and other Churches of Christ that are off-shoots of the Boston Church of Christ, and The Family (originally known as the Children of God). There has also been some sensationalist reporting of alleged satanic abuse but, as in the USA, the stories turn out to be fabrications, unproven or the result of 'ordinary' child abuse or paedophilia, rather than the result of satanic beliefs. There is certainly no evidence that a network of satanists is carrying out the ritual rape and murder that has been alleged in some quarters.

There are, however, literally hundreds of other NRMs in Britain, whose presence passes unnoticed by the general public and whose members are at least as law-abiding and 'ordinary' as their fellow citizens. In a short paper, it is impossible even to begin to describe the diversity of the movements, but the point cannot be overstressed that NRMs in Britain, as elsewhere, should not be 'lumped together', and that it should never be assumed that what is true of one movement is necessarily true of any other.

Definitions

There are three terms used in Britain to cover the phenomena referred to in this paper: new religious movements (NRMs), sects and cults. There is no agreement about what is meant by any of these terms, or, indeed, which movements should be included or excluded. Being firmly of the conviction that concepts are more or less useful, rather than more or less true, I have no intention of entering the taxonomic debate in this paper, but a few brief remarks might help to clarify the confusion that exists.[6]

New Religious Movement (NRM)

The term 'new religious movement' is the one most frequently employed by scholars. While this avoids the evaluative overtones associated in the mind of the general public with the term 'cult', it is not ideal. It is sometimes objected that many of the movements are not new or that they are not religious. Most NRMs are, however, new in the sense that they became visible in their present form since the Second World War; thus, although a movement such as the International Society for Krishna Consciousness (ISKCON) will trace its roots back 500 years or more, it is new in that its Western institutional form did not exist before His Divine Grace A.C. Bhaktivedanta Prabhupada founded it in the US in the 1960s; and although SUBUD was originally founded in the 1930s, it was unknown in Britain until its leader, the Indonesian Muhammad Subuh Sumohadiwidjojo, came to Britain in 1957. Despite the fact that much of the Human Potential movement, some New Age groups and even certain Hindu-based movements such as the Science of Creative Intelligence (Transcendental Meditation) and the Brahma Kumaris will deny that they are religions, these may be called religious (in the admittedly rather wide) sense that they offer answers or solutions to fundamental or ultimate questions such as 'What is the purpose or meaning of life, or of the nature of things?', 'Why am I here?' or 'How can I acquire transcendent knowledge, spiritual enlightenment, or self-realisation?'

The term NRM, thus defined, may include not only movements such as the Unification Church, the Church of Scientology, Sahaja Yoga and the Rajneeshees, but also New Age and Neo-Pagan groups, witches' covens and 'self-religions' such as INSIGHT, the Forum, Exegesis and Silva Mind Control. The term NRM is sometimes also used to refer to groups that are affiliated with or part of older traditions, such as Opus Dei, the Neo-Catechumenates or some of the House Churches (some of which now refer to themselves as the New Churches), because they may display certain characteristics (such as strictly held beliefs and authoritarian control over members) that are associated with some of the more controversial constituents of the category NRM.

Cult

In popular parlance, the term 'cult' is used to cover roughly the same spectrum of movements as those referred to as NRMs. Here, 'cult' or 'destructive cult', especially as used by the more sensationalist media and the anti-cultists, is usually taken to imply a motley assortment of negative characteristics such as bizarre and heretical beliefs, brainwashing and mind control, financial exploitation and malpractice, political manipulation and intrigue, deceptive practices, sexual orgies and individual or mass suicide — the sins of one being attributed to all.

Scholars may also use the term 'cult', but they do so in a technical sense by way of contrast with other technically defined usages of 'sect', 'church' and/or 'denomination',[7] and they would be likely to refer to religions such as Jehovah's Witnesses, Christian Science, the Church of Jesus Christ of Latter-day Saints (the Mormons) and Seventh-day Adventism as nineteenth century sects, or as recently formed denominations, while anti-cultists are more likely to include such religions in their list of cults.[8]

Numbers[9]

The number of NRMs does, of course, depend on the definition that is used, and on decisions such as whether individual New Age groups or House/New Churches are counted separately or together. By 1997, INFORM (see below) had some sort of information on computer about the existence of around 2,500 groups or movements in Britain, and it also held further information about various other small groups, most of which advertise themselves through the New Age or Human Potential media. The figure of 2,600 will be an underestimate of the total number in that there are bound to be groups not known to INFORM, but this might be balanced by the fact that some of the groups which are single 'congregations' may also be part of a wider network and so, according to different accounting criteria, may be 'really' only a sub-group.

Numbers of members are even more difficult to estimate as many of the movements either exaggerate or do not want to reveal their membership figures. The problem is compounded by the fact that anti-cultists have tended to disseminate grossly exaggerated numbers, not least because they wish to underline the potential threat of the movements to society. Allied to this, anti-cultists, like the NRMs (who do not wish to publicise the fact that converts frequently become disillusioned with the movement), will tend to ignore, or even deny, the very high turn-over rates (*their* reason being that these rates question the oft-repeated, but demonstrably false, assertion that the 'destructive cults' use techniques of 'brainwashing', mind control or psychological coercion that are irresistible and irreversible.[10]

Moreover, just as the uncertainty about exactly what constitutes an NRM exacerbates the uncertainty about the number of movements, so does the uncertainty about what constitutes membership of a movement exacerbate the uncertainty of how many members there are: degrees of involvement range from complete dedication of one's life to a movement (with, perhaps, little or no contact with non-members), to the occasional, brief visit to a centre or the taking of a one-off course and then having no further contact — although the movement itself may count such a person as a member from then on (as would be the case with the Church of Scientology). Indeed, several movements may count the same individual as one of their members, especially within the 'self-religions', Human Potential movement or New Age networks where members, 'graduates' and/or 'clients' tend to try out a number of different philosophies and techniques. A further complication is that many of the members of NRMs now have children, some even have grandchildren, born into their movement. If these children are counted, as Catholics would count them, as members (rather than if, like Baptists, we were to wait for an adult commitment of faith to be made), the numbers will be considerably increased.

Given these qualifications, let me, nonetheless, risk offering an albeit crude estimate of the numbers of people involved in NRMs in Britain, a country which (to put the figures in perspective) has a total population of 57 million, of whom roughly 80% are aged 16 or over.

Few, if any, of the movements have succeeded, at any one time, in accumulating more than a few hundred persons who devote their whole lives to working for the movement, making no more than a few thousand such members in total. It is probable that the number of people who, while living in their own homes and being employed in an 'outside' job, are deeply committed and devote almost all of their spare time to a particular group or movement would reach several tens of thousands.[11] A greater number of people, perhaps a few hundred thousand, maintain a more peripheral relationship, which may, none the less, be of considerable importance in their lives. A far greater number will have come into contact with one or another of the movements for a short, transitory period, with possibly a million or more having gone as far as to participate in a seminar, course or workshop or to spend at least several hours investigating an NRM. There could be two or three million of the adult population who have, minimally, 'dabbled in' or 'flirted with' one or other of the movements in Britain at some time during the past quarter-century.

The point to be stressed is that, although some hundreds of thousands of individuals may have been classified as a 'member' of an NRM at some time during the past quarter of a century, the numbers of people whose involvement in an NRM results in their having greatly reduced contact with the rest of the world because they are living in a centre or working full-time for a movement, is, at any one time, very small, involving what is probably well under one per cent of the adult population in Britain.

But it is to make a complementary, not a contradictory, point to say that there could be several millions of Britons who have been affected in some way by the beliefs and practices of some of the movements, even though many of them may never have had direct contact with an NRM. The media, particularly television, not infrequently incorporate information in programmes, and thus the general 'cultural milieu' is imbued with ideas not normally associated with mainstream British Christianity. One belief which doubtless owes some of its extraordinary spread in recent years to NRMs (as well as to immigration, travel and the media) is the doctrine of reincarnation — indeed, a new quarterly magazine *Reincarnation International* has recently appeared. By 1990, 24% of Britons (compared to 20% in an aggregate of other European countries) were claiming that they believed in reincarnation (interestingly, 32% of Catholics in the sample said they believed in reincarnation).[12]

Perhaps the confusion that sometimes arises about what exactly is meant by membership and, relatedly, about the numbers of people 'involved' in the movements can be further illustrated by looking in a bit more detail at the different kinds of involvement that exist in two movements that have had a relatively large number of people associated with them at some point: Transcendental Meditation (TM) and the Church of Scientology.

Transcendental Meditation's Office of Information and Inspiration tells me that by 1997, 180,000 people in Britain have learned TM during a 4-day course, with about 5,000 more taking the course every year. A total of around 3,200 have proceeded to the advanced 'TM-Sidhi Programme'. Most of these people continue to lead 'ordinary lives' in that they neither work for nor reside with the movement, although an unknown number of them devote some time to meditation each day. However, some of those who practice the advanced TM-Sidhi Programme, while remaining in outside jobs, have moved to live in the movement's 'Ideal Village' in Skelmersdale, Lancashire, which has around 400 residents and a day school for about 100 of the residents' children. About 550-600 Meditators have pursued the techniques to train as TM teachers; of these, about 50-60 have a full-time career as TM teachers and a further 60 or so are teaching on a part-time basis. About 40 people are engaged in various projects at Mentmore Towers, a further 8 or so are 'working for charity' at the movement's residential academy in Kent. Altogether there are around 100 people working full-time for TM in Britain.

The Church of Scientology reports that, since it had started offering courses in Britain in the early 1950s, between one and two hundred thousand people have paid for at least one of their introductory courses, which normally take place over a weekend. Currently (1997), they say that about 1,000 people in the UK take a course each year. Only a very small proportion of these people end up devoting their lives to the movement, which now has 330 full-time staff members at its headquarters in East Grinstead, and about 290 further staff members in other centres around the country. There is a drug rehabilitation centre near Tunbridge Wells where people use the Narconon Programme; and an independent school, Greenfields, uses the Study Technology developed by L. Ron Hubbard for subjects up to and including A-Level.

Turning to a few of the other better-known NRMs, the *Unification Church*, which has been in England since the late 1960s, has in 1997 about 1,000 core members in Britain (roughly seventy per cent of whom are British). This number would be doubled if children of Unification parents were included. *The Family* (formerly the

Children of God) says that it now has about 47 full-time adult members, with about 83 children; there are 'Turf Supporters' (65 adults and 167 children who, although not totally committed to leading the demanding missionary life of Family members, do, nonetheless, accept most of the beliefs and keep in close touch with the movement).

ISKCON (the 'Hare Krishna' movement) has initiated about 960 devotees in Britain (at a present rate of 40 - 50 *per annum*); of these initiates, 3-400 are still actively involved (207 living in ISKCON temples or residences, but only about 50 working full-time for the movement). There is a growing number of children in the movement, born to around 50 families, with about 40 children attending the ISKCON school to the north-west of London. There are also 29 groups of *Nama Hatta* or 450 associate members, and about 4,200 Patrons who, having given a donation, receive the *Back to Godhead* magazine and may visit their nearest temple. A similar pattern is to be found with the 10,000 or so followers of Sathya *Sai Baba*, but as the overwhelming majority belong to the Asian community, rather than Anglo-Saxon Britons (of whom there may be a few hundred), they, like the Krishna devotees of Asian origin, tend not to be considered 'cult members' — for no very rational reason.[13]

Several tens, if not hundreds of thousands of Britons will have had contact with the *Rajneeshee* organization at some time, and many went to either Poona, in India, or Rajneeshpuram, in Oregon, USA, in the past. At the present time, there are an estimated 2,500 - 3,000 people associated with the movement in Britain,[14] and it has its own school, Ko Hsuan, with 16 staff and 52 boarders, in north Devon. A spokesman for *Elan Vital* (previously the Divine Light Mission) has said that around 25,000 persons have 'received the Knowledge' in Britain, with about 2,000 regular attendees at the 'presentations' (that have, to some extent, taken the place of *satsang*); there are two full-time workers for the movement, assisted by a few volunteers. *Sahaja Yoga* has around 300 members who practice on a regular basis, with roughly two-thirds of these regularly attending meetings. *Ananda Marga* has had a presence in Britain for a number of years, but it keeps a fairly low profile, with four full-time margiis, a further 26 active members, a few score peripheral participants and a few hundred 'transitory associates'. The *Brahma Kumaris* first opened a centre in Britain in 1971. There are now 45 centres (some of which may be little more than an apartment) in the UK. About 1,000 'students' are said to meditate daily, with about 70 working for the movement on a full-time basis.

Sōka Gakkai International UK was originally introduced into Britain in the early 1960s as Nichiren Shōshū UK.[15] It now has about four thousand members who have received their Gohonzon,[16] but no more than ten full-time staff members. While there are about 6,000 'Friends' of the FWBO (*Friends of the Western Buddhist Order*), there are only 350 active, ordained members currently in Britain, 150 of whom work for the Order full-time. A *Mahikari* group was founded in Britain in 1983. Just over 1,000 have attended one or more of the talks that they have been giving to the public during the past five years, and there is an active membership of between 2-300.

Landmark Education claims that 17,000 have 'graduated' in Britain from the Erhard Seminar Trainings (*est*) or the *Forum*, which now holds 3-day-and-one-evening-long Seminars for 1-200 persons every two or three months in London. The fee of £235 includes the Forum in Action Seminar of eight evenings. Graduates may then go on to take the Landmark Advanced and/or the Communication courses, and some will continue training to the point of becoming a Forum Leader, but many keep in touch for special evenings and may help as volunteers in the office or during a Seminar — and it is quite likely that a significant proportion of the 17,000 are individuals who had already done the Seminar but decided to do it again as a 'refresher course'.[17] *Life Training* claims that 4,000 have done at least one of their courses, with 400 regularly participating in courses. There are two full-time and one part-time paid workers. Other movements such as *Insight/MSIA* (for which it is suggested that participants pay £350 for three evenings, a weekend and a follow up evening), *Psychosynthesis, Rebirthing, Outlook Seminar Training* (previously known as *I am Grove*) and *Self-Transformation Seminars* may have had roughly 5-12,000 doing one of their courses. As elsewhere, several human development organizations (including TM) offer their courses not merely to individuals but also to a number of business corporations, where middle and upper management are exposed to new ways of conceptualising and relating to themselves and their colleagues.

Some local social services and at least one British prison are also making use of such services.[18]

There are about 150 *Emissaries of Divine Light*, 60 of whom live in their Cotswold community. Yogi Bhajan came to Britain in the early 1970s and now *3HO* (the Healthy, Happy, Holy Organization) Kundalini Yoga Foundation has six Kundalini teachers in the country, all of whom hold down other, outside, work; its mailing list is 300-strong, and about 60 people regularly attend events. Between 1,200 and 1,400 people are said to practice the 'latihan' twice a week with fellow members of *Subud*. There were about 300 names on the *Raëlian's* mailing list in 1988, but reportedly only a few were committed followers.[19] More recently (1997), the movement has claimed that it has over 500 sympathisers, of whom 50 or so regularly attend meetings. About 650 people have received *ECKANKAR* literature, and about 4-500 attend the movement's major events. The *Free Daist* organization of 'Heart Master' *Da Avabhasa* (a.k.a. *Da Free John*) came to Britain in 1984. It now has a mailing list of about 100. There are 50 practitioners and, in 1997, 12 novices; living in Da Avabhasa Ashram in Norwich, is a core group of 10 members, of whom three are full-time missionaries.

The *Pagan Federation*, which was founded in 1971 and claims to be the largest and oldest Pagan and Wicca body in Europe,[20] estimates that it has 4-5,000 members in the UK, about 70 per cent of whom may be described as 'committed'. An as-yet-unsubstantiated claim has been made that there is 'a conservative estimated population of over 250,000 *Witches/Pagans* throughout the UK and many more hundreds of thousands of people with a serious interest in Astrology, Alternative Healing Techniques and Psychic Powers',[21] but the Pagan Federation estimate is that there are around 100,000 Pagens in the UK.

Indigenous NRMs

The vast majority of NRMs in Britain were introduced from other countries — mostly from the East, particularly India, or from North America, particularly California — through (a) immigration, (b) Britons returning after learning about an NRM while abroad, or (c) the efforts of overseas missionaries. No attempt is being made in this paper to describe the beliefs and practices of such movements as the information is readily available elsewhere.[22] There are, however, a number of movements which were founded in Britain. These range from Evangelical Christian to esoteric and Neo-Pagan groups and include a large number of New Age organizations, and in this section I shall give a brief introduction to some of the better-known of these organizations.

The *Jesus Fellowship* or *Jesus Army* was founded when members of the local Bugbrooke Baptist Church set up a community in 1969. Its expansion beyond the local community and the strict beliefs and practices adopted by the group led to adverse publicity and the separation of the growing movement from the Baptist Union of Great Britain. In recent years, the Fellowship has achieved a high profile and enjoyed some success in persuading young people (including a number of 'down and outs') to join them; they have also organized joint campaigns with some of the more fervently evangelistic House Church groups.[23] The Fellowship now (1997) has around 2,500 members, 900 of whom live in its 60 community households.

The School of Economic Science (SES) was originally created by Andrew MacLaren (1883-1982) as a small group to study economic phenomena and the 'underlying Natural Law'. MacLaren's son, Leonardo da Vinci (Leon), was to become its leader and to introduce to the movement the thought of Gurdjieff and Ouspensky and then, in the late 1950s through the influence of Maharishi Mahesh Yogi, the Hindu tradition that arose out of the ninth-century philosopher, Shankara. Professional people tend to be disproportionately attracted to the SES, first to attend a series of classes, but later, to devote most of their leisure time to activities associated with the movement. Apart from advertising its courses on the London Underground transport system, the SES has tried to keep a low profile. It, and the 'ordinary' schools which it runs, have, however, been the subject of some public controversy — especially after London's evening newspaper, *The Standard*, published some exposé articles, which were later elaborated into a book.[24] At that time (1984), the Principal of the *School of Economic Science* is reported to have said that 'the Fellowship of the School amounted to about 120 people... [and] that there were probably about 2,500 general SES members in London, and the same number again elsewhere in the country'. The SES is also reported to have claimed that some 50,000 people had been through its doors since it was started.[25]

Exegesis is a 'self-religion' not unlike *est*, that was founded by Robert D'Aubigny (formerly Robert Fuller) in 1976, but which ceased to operate in 1984. However, D'Aubigny also set up a telephone marketing agency under the name of *Programmes Ltd* in 1981; this is still active, and operates on the principles propagated in the Exegesis Seminars. Around 6,000 persons went through the *Exegesis* seminar, with the subsequent activities of Programmes possibly adding a further 1,000 graduates.[26] *Lifewave* was a movement started in 1974 by John Yarr, who had been initiated into the Divine Light Mission. Yarr gathered followers around him from England and the movement spread to other parts of the world, but in 1986 Lifewave was disbanded as the result of a number of sexual scandals.[27] The *Aetherius Society* was founded in London in 1955 by George King, who claims to be in touch with a number of Cosmic Beings, some of whom have come to earth in UFOs or flying saucers.[28] Representatives of the Society claim that 5,000 people have contact with them, with several hundred being committed supporters. There are four paid and six unpaid full-time workers, with a further 30 or so volunteers. There are a dozen centres throughout England, and between 50 and 80 people attend the Sunday service. The journal *Cosmic Voice* and *The Aetherius Society Newsletter* have a circulation of around 700.

The *Emin Foundation* is an esoteric group that was founded in London in 1973 by Raymond Armin, known to his followers as Leo. The movement has spread to places as far away as the USA and New Zealand, and there is an Emin kibbutz in Israel. On Saturday, 24 April 1982, the London *Times* carried a full-page advertisement declaring that 'THE CHRIST IS NOW HERE'. The advertisement was placed by *The Tara Press*, an organization founded to propagate the teachings of Benjamin Creme, a Scotsman living in London who claims to have been receiving messages about the coming of Maitreya since the late 1950s. Creme's group, founded in 1974, publishes a magazine *Share International* with a circulation of 300 or so, which expounds on the esoteric teachings of the Maitreya. Creme holds regular meetings in London which are attended by roughly 100 people, including 50 or so 'regulars'. He has also travelled around the world, disseminating information about the Maitreya, and there is now a

Tara Centre in the United States, with representatives in Australia and 'much interest' in India. Creme's pronouncements owe much to the teachings of Alice Bailey, and have a certain amount in common with the Bailey-inspired *Lucis Trust*, a London-based organization that incorporates the *Arcane School*, *Triangles* and *World Goodwill*.

Thee Temple ov [sic] *Psychic Youth (TOPY)* came into existence in 1981, largely due to the efforts of the pop musician, Genesis P Orrige. 'Templars' believed that self-improvement was the responsibility of individuals; they were anti-dogma, anti-bureaucracy, anti-'absolute Truth', and strongly influenced by the thought of William Burroughs and Aleister Crowley. Ritual sex magick was their means of liberating inherent 'energy' or 'power'. In 1992, following a police raid on *TOPY* headquarters, the movement was disbanded. The *Process* Church of the Final Judgment was a satanic organization, founded in London in 1963. It moved to America and it also seemed to have disbanded, but there have been reports that it, or a splinter group, is operating in Europe and, perhaps, in Britain.[29]

The *Findhorn Foundation*, a New Age community in the north of Scotland, was founded by Peter and Eileen Caddy and Dorothy Maclean in 1962. About 200 people live in the community, but an estimated 8 - 10,000 Britons and others from around the world visit Findhorn each year, many participating in the 'Experience Week' or one of the other courses that the Foundation offers.[30] Findhorn has close connections with the international network of New Agers, exchanging speakers with Esalen in California and elsewhere. It also has close ties with *Alternatives*, an organization that arranges talks on a variety of New Age and other alternative philosophies on Monday evenings at St James's Church, Piccadilly, in the heart of London's West End.

Like most European countries, the United Kingdom has its own rich tradition upon which to draw for the more pagan elements of its New Age. There are Celtic gods and goddesses who were shared under different names by a number of European cultures, but some have survived — or been revived — as English, Scottish, Irish and/or Welsh in their territorial allegiance.[31] The Druids too, whether or not they were really connected with Stonehenge, have certainly claimed an ancient heritage of English soil — modern Druidism can be traced to the eighteenth century in both Wales and England.[32] Other ancient monuments, standing stones and numerous ley lines have waited thousands of years for a popular sacredness to be reinvested — be it at Avebury, or Glastonbury (one of the sites of the celebration of the Harmonic Convergence), or Pilgrim Street in the City of London. These and other historical sites and myths have provided some of the resources from which numerous groups have drawn in developing a large variety of Neo-pagan associations, Magick circles, witches' covens and New Age/Healing groups which are too numerous even to begin to list, but the catalogues of meetings, seminars, workshops and 'happenings' advertised in magazines such as *Pagan Voice*, *Creation Spirituality*, *Kindred Spirit*, *Rainbow Ark*, *i to i*, *Prediction*, *Human Potential* or *Leading Edge* leave no doubt in the reader's mind that, for those seeking alternative ways, there is a veritable cornucopia of choice on offer in Britain.[33]

NRMs — the State and the Law

England and Scotland both have established Churches (the Church in Wales was disestablished in 1930). Unlike the United States and various other nations, Britain has no written Constitution with provisions conserving fundamental human rights and freedoms. There are some *laws* giving rights and protections (such as the 1944 Education Act, the 1970 Equal Pay Act which obliges women to be paid the same wage as men for the same job, and the 1976 Race Relations Act which forbids discrimination on the grounds of race), but there are no laws in Britain protecting the rights of religious minorities. Ironically, Northern Ireland is the only place within the United Kingdom where discrimination on the basis of religion is unlawful. Although the United Kingdom is a party to the European Convention on Human Rights and Fundamental Freedoms, its laws are not always in conformity with some of the Convention's provisions, and there is a strong difference of opinion about the desirability of incorporating the Convention into British domestic law. Nonetheless:

Everyone in Britain has the right to religious freedom (in teaching, worship and observance) without interference from the community or the State. Churches and other religious societies may own property, run schools, and promote their views in speech and writing. There is no religious bar to the holding of public office, although ministers of the

Church of England and the Church of Scotland may not become Members of Parliament.[34]

In other words, British citizens may embrace, practice and promote whatever beliefs they wish, so long as they do not perform criminal acts; and, as far as legal status is concerned, NRMs enjoy as much (or little) as other non-established religions. They may, furthermore, apply for charitable status, and several of them have acquired this, thus gaining exemption from certain taxes.

There have, however, been instances where the NRMs have (in some cases understandably) considered themselves to be the victims of Governmental or legal discrimination. In 1968, although there was no power under existing law to prohibit the practice of Scientology, the Government concluded that the Church 'is so objectionable that it would be right to take all steps within their power to curb its growth'.[35] Foreign nationals were no longer to be eligible to enter Britain as students or employees of the movement. The 1971 Foster Report on the Church of Scientology concluded that although Scientology establishments might not come under the description of 'bona fide educational establishments', it seemed wrong not to allow visitors entry because they were proposing to do something that it was legal for Britons to do.[36] In 1974, a Dutch woman was refused entry and the case was taken to the European Court of Justice, which ruled that the United Kingdom was entitled, for reasons of public policy, to refuse the right of entry to a national of another member State. The ban on Scientology entry remained in force for twelve years; then three reasons were given for its removal: (a) it was unenforceable because Scientologists did not need to declare themselves as such on entering the country; (b) it might be difficult to defend before the European Court of Human Rights at Strasbourg; and (c), it was unfair, since Scientology was the only movement for which Britain's general religious tolerance was thus suspended.

The most publicised and significant court case involving an NRM in Britain made history as the longest civil action in Britain. This was the libel suit which the Unification Church brought and lost against a national tabloid, the *Daily Mail*. As well as finding for the defendant, the jury requested that the movement should have its charitable status removed. There followed a long investigation, with the matter eventually being dropped due to insufficient evidence. It is impossible to assess the full consequences of the *Daily Mail* case and the fact that the jury had recommended the withdrawal of charitable status, but there can be little doubt that life for the movement became considerably more difficult. To take just one example: the jury's decision was used as the reason for a Local Authority to dismiss a Unification play-group leader because she was 'not a fit person to look after children', despite the fact that there was no evidence that she had not done her job well and, indeed, many of the parents testified that her work had been excellent.[37] Other incidents involving the Unification Church and the law include several minor offences (concerning pedlars' licences and charges of obstruction), and the rejection of an application by the movement to grant a *habeas corpus* request when one of its members, a 28-year-old woman, was being held against her will by a professional deprogrammer.[38]

One of the longest-running cases to hit the headlines concerns the Hertsmere Borough Council's decision to ban the use of Bhaktivedanta Manor (a large mansion bought by the Beatle George Harrison for ISKCON) for festivals or public worship. The ban came into force in March 1994, but, in May 1996 permission was granted by the Secretary of State for the Environment for an access road which will bypass the village of Letchmore Heath and allow public worship at the Manor. Other NRMs have been involved in libel and custody cases, when membership of a movement has been argued to be a reason to give custody to the non-member parent.

So far as the mainstream Churches are concerned, there are individual members of the Churches (including clergy) who have taken a number of diverse positions, either supporting or attacking NRMs, but the hierarchies have made few public pronouncements about the movements. They have, however, officially supported INFORM (see below) both financially and politically, endorsing its position as set out in *New Religious Movements: A Practical Introduction.*[39]

Groups Concerned with NRMs

There are several 'anti-cult' or 'cult-watching' groups in Britain. FAIR (Family Action Information and Rescue) — recently changed to 'Resource' — was founded in 1975 by Paul Rose,who was at that time a Labour Member of Parliament and who was successfully sued for libel by the Unification Church. FAIR has a number of local branches throughout the country, and it produces a quarterly newsletter which contains reports on cult activities, often reproduced from the media or anti-cult literature in other countries. Although it is officially against the practice of forcible deprogramming, FAIR has had deprogrammers sitting on its committee, and its past chairman, the late Lord Rodney, employed a deprogrammer to 'rescue' his daughter from a movement. It has an annual meeting, attended mainly by parents and ex-members, at which Americans including Margaret Singer, Steven Hassan, Cynthia Kissinger and Patricia Ryan have been speakers. FAIR is closely associated with a Parent Support Group which also holds meetings at which ex-members and others may give talks. Around the mid-1980s, some members of FAIR became dissatisfied with what they considered was the insufficiently robust attitude of some of its committee and a breakaway group, *Cultists Anonymous (CA)* was formed. However, following the exodus of the more moderate members of FAIR, Lord Rodney, one of CA's founding members was asked to become FAIR's chairman, and, more recently, the two groups have merged, FAIR taking over a 24-hour 'cult hot-line' that CA had installed.

The *Deo Gloria Trust* is one of several evangelical groups that have produced literature 'exposing the cults'. It was founded by a wealthy businessman, Kenneth Frampton, whose sons had joined the Children of God, but since his death it has had a much lower profile. Other evangelical groups include the *Reachout Trust* which has a newsletter that included discussions about 'wrong beliefs' such as those held by Mormons, Jehovah's Witnesses, the New Age, and Roman Catholics. It was the Reachout Trust that was largely responsible for advertising the dangers of Satanism and an outcrop of alleged cases of ritual child abuse in Britain towards the end of the 1980s. *Christian Information Outreach* publishes a small quarterly, *Awareness*, which, like the Reachout Trust, is as concerned about Jehovah's Witnesses and Mormons and Roman Catholics as it is about the Occult, Pantheism and religions from the East. The *Cult Information Centre* (CIC) was set up in Britain in the late 1980s by Ian Haworth, who, after spending a few days doing a course with PSI (People Searching Inside), had set himself up as a cult expert in the Toronto-based anti-cult group, COMA. The CIC is basically a one-man operation, but others have been employed by Haworth, including, at one time, an ex-Unificationist,

Jane Allison, who has since been involved in deprogramming activities.[40]

These groups have some contact with each other, but attempts to work together have not been very successful, mainly because of the different interests and attitudes of the memberships. FAIR, CA, and the CIC do, however, work together insofar as they advise enquirers to use the same telephone hot-line, and they are all in regular communication with the international anti-cult network.

Several organizations have been founded by some of the NRMs themselves (e.g. the Church of Scientology and the Unification Church) for the purpose of protecting their religious freedoms, but none of these has received much in the way of outside support, and most have faded away after a short period.

According to its own literature, the *SAFF* (Sub-Culture Alternatives Freedom Foundation) was founded:

as a result of donations sent in by well-wishers following the fire-bombing of a Leeds New Age bookstore (The Sorcerer's Apprentice) by religious fanatics. (Its aims are) to protect the right of ALL individuals to be able to pursue and further their own particular beliefs, religious proclivities, cultural style and world views...[41]

SAFF does not, however, appear to have had much impact and may have disappeared altogether.

In 1988, George Chryssides, who teaches at the University of Wolverhampton, founded the *Council for Religious Freedom*, a group of members of NRMs and of longer-established religions and a few academics who share a concern about preserving religious freedom in all areas of British society. By 1995, however, the Council had virtually ceased to exist.

There are other organizations that are interested in the NRMs, but which differ from the above-mentioned groups in that they are more interested in collecting accurate information than in lobbying either for or against the movements — although none of them would deny that the public ought to be alerted to the potential dangers associated with some of the movements (and, indeed, some anti-cult activities). The Centre for New Religious Movements *(CENERM)* was founded in 1981, when Dr Harold Turner moved his vast collection of data about PRINERMS (NRMs that have developed in primal societies) from Aberdeen to the Selly Oak Colleges in Birmingham. CENERM still specializes in

PRINERMS, but, under the Directorship of Dr Jack Thompson (who has now moved to the University of Edinburgh), it started collecting information about NRMs in the West. *The Centre for New Religious Movements* was started at King's College, London in 1982 by Professor Stewart Sutherland, and is now directed by Dr Peter Clarke. The Centre has a large collection of information about NRMs and organises conferences at which academics can report on research, and members or practitioners can explain their beliefs and practices. The Centre also publishes *The Journal of Contemporary Religion* (former *Religion Today*) three times a year. The *Housetop Centre* for Christian Resources, directed by Dr John Wijngaards, MHM, is a Roman Catholic charity which began in London in 1983 to provide information about NRMs and to offer counselling to relatives and friends of members of NRMs, and to those who are or have themselves been in a movement.

INFORM (Information Network Focus on Religious Movements), which I founded in 1988 with support from the Government and mainstream Churches, is an independent, non-sectarian charity that aims to help people by providing objective up-to-date information about NRMs.[42] As well as dealing with personal enquiries by mail, telephone and through visits to its offices (housed at the London School of Economics), it has produced literature including leaflets on the movements and a book, which summarises academic research in as far as this might be of practical use, as well as offering suggestions about how friends, relatives, teachers, clergy, counsellors or other professions might appproach a situation in which someone has joined an NRM.[43]

INFORM also puts on day-long Seminars twice a year for a nation-wide network to whom it may refer enquirers for specialist knowledge, and pastoral or counselling skills. In March 1993, INFORM organized a 4-day conference on New Religions and the New Europe which was attended by over 200 participants from 23 different societies. The proceedings were opened with a talk by Earl Ferrers, Minister of State at the Home Office; most of the speakers were scholars, but two panels were made up of, in one case, half a dozen representatives of NRMs and, in the other, of representatives of several 'cult-watching groups'. INFORM has also devoted some time to training a small, London-based group of professional counsellors about the NRMs and discussing with them cases of individuals or families affected by a movement (being careful, always, to preserve confidentiality). A growing number of undergraduates and even school children have also become engaged in writing short dissertations or essays on one or more of the movements, many of them contacting INFORM for factual information.

Concluding Remarks

Britain does not seem to be fundamentally different from other countries in the West as far as NRMs are concerned. It is, however, possible that it has more movements per capita than average, and that the number of groups interested in the movements is slightly greater than is common elsewhere, with an unusually high proportion of these groups and a high proportion of academic scholars being interested in objective studies. While not exactly exhibiting enthusiasm for the NRMs, the Government and the mainstream churches, as instituitions, have been careful not to discriminate against the movements and their members. Some discrimination can be observed in the courts, sections of the media and in the attitudes of sections of the general public, but there is no evidence to suggest that this is more than the kind of treatment that is meted out to some other minorities in the society. Some of the movements have given rise to genuine difficulties for the society,[44] but the vast majority of movements and their members are perhaps best regarded as contemporary manifestations of a gently secularizing pluralistic democracy.[45]

Notes

1. See Bernice Martin, *A Sociology of Contemporary Cultural Change*, Oxford: Blackwell, 1981, for a perceptive account of the British youth culture within which NRMs emerged in Britain.
2. See Eileen Barker, 'New Religious Movements in Britain: The Context and the Membership', *Social Compass*, Vol. 30:1, 1983: 33-48.
3. See James A. Beckford, 'The Public Response to New Religious Movements in Britain' *Social Compass*, Vol. 30:1, 1983: 49-62, *Cult Controversies: The Societal Response to New Religious Movements*, London: Tavistock, 1985, and Eileen Barker, *The Making of a Moonie: Brainwashing or Choice?* Aldershot: Gregg Revivals, 1993, pp. 121 & 129 (originally published by Blackwell, Oxford, 1984).

4. See Eileen Barker, *New Religious Movements: A Practical Introduction*, London: HMSO, 1989, especially ch. 11 and Appendix III for further information about deprogramming.

5. For example, the BBC programme, *Panorama*, showed a deprogrammer and his, in this case, unsuccessfully treated, Scientology 'subject' in April 1987; and on Thames Television, 6 August 1990, *The Cooke Report* showed two deprogrammings (one 'successful', one not) of members of the London Church of Christ.

6. I go into a fuller discussion of definitions and the uses to which they are put in Eileen Barker 'But is it a Genuine Religion?' in Thomas Robbins and Arthur Greil (eds.) *Between Sacred and Secular: Research and Theory on Quasi-religion*, Greenwich, Conn. : JAI Press, 1994: 97-125; and, to a lesser extent, in Eileen Barker, *New Religious Movements: A Practical Introduction*, London: HMSO, 1989, especially pp. 4-6, and 145-48.

7. See, for example, Roy Wallis, 'Scientology: Therapeutic Cult to Religious Sect', *Sociology*, 9, 1975: 89-100; and Rodney Stark & William Sims Bainbridge, *The Future of Religion: Secularization, Revival and Cult Formation*, Berkeley : University of California Press, 1985, ch. 2.

8. There are some evangelical Protestant groups, such as Christian Information Outreach and the Reachout Trust, which would include mainstream Roman Catholicism in their list of cults.

9. I would like to thank Michelle Pauli for her help in updating the statistics in this paper.

10. In my study of the Unification Church, I found that the majority of members left of their own free will within two years of joining (see *The Making of a Moonie: Brainwashing or Choice?* Aldershot: Gregg Revivals, 1993: 146). See Eileen Barker, *New Religious Movements: A Practical Introduction*, London: HMSO, 1989: 104-5 for a more general discussion of rates of voluntary defection. See David Bromley (ed.), *Falling from the Faith: Causes and Consequences of Religious Apostasy*, London: Sage, 1988, Parts I & III, for a comparative analysis and further references about people leaving NRMs.

11. In 1985, James Beckford estimated that there had never been more than 15,000 committed members in Britain at any point in the previous decade (*Cult Controversies*, London: Tavistock, 1985: 244.)

12. Gallup *European Values Survey*, 1990. At the time of writing, these data were not yet available to the public, and I am grateful for the opportunity to have seen them.

13. David Bowen, *The Sathya Sai Baba Community in Bradford: Its Origins and Development, Religious Beliefs and Practices*, Department of Theology and Religious Studies, University of Leeds, Community Religions Project, 1988.

14. This estimation comes from Elizabeth Puttick's as yet unpublished PhD thesis on the movement.

15. The number of registered members in Britain is about 6,000, with perhaps 4,500 chanting more or less regularly. There are around one dozen full-time staff members.

16. Bryan Wilson and Karel Dobbelaere, *A Time to Chant: The Sōka Gakkai Buddhists in Britain*, Oxford: Clarendon Press, 1994: 3, 39.

17. When I did the Seminar in February 1994, there were at least twelve persons who had attended it before, and I spoke to five who had attended more times.

18. Several of these estimates owe much to discussions with Dr Paul Heelas of the University of Lancaster, who has studied the 'self-religions' for several years. Other information not specifically referenced comes from enquiries made in 1992-93 by INFORM for Peter Brierley's, *UK Christian Handbook 1994/95 Edition*, London Christian Research Association et al., 1993, or by myself in March 1994, through direct contact with the movements concerned. See also Rodney Stark and W.S. Bainbridge, *The Future of Religion: Secularization, Revival and Cult Formation*, Berkeley: University of California Press, 1985, for a discussion of NRM statistics comparing North America with Western Europe.

19. Alan Yeo, 'Is There Anybody Out There?', *Midweek*, 28 July 1988.

20. Vivianne Crowley, *Phoenix from the Flame: Pagan Spirituality in the Western World*, London: Aquarian Press, 1994: 259.

21. Chris Bray, *The Occult Census: Statistical Analysis and Results*, Leeds: The Sorcerer's Apprentice Press, 1989: 3.

22. The Institute for the Study of American Religion (ISAR) is undoubtedly the best source of data about NRMs. Its Director, J. Gordon Melton, has produced a vast number of reference books on the subject, among the most useful for background reading about the 'multi-national' NRMs are his *Encyclopedia of American Religions* (4th ed.), Detroit: Gale, 1993; *Encyclopedic Handbook of Cults in America*, Revised and updated edition New York: Garland, 1992; and *New Age Encyclopedia*, Detroit: Gale, 1990.

23. Simon Cooper and Mike Farrant, with contributions from other members including the movement's leader, Noel Stanton, offer an insiders' perspective in *Fire in Our Hearts: The Story of the Jesus Fellowship*, Eastbourne: Kingsway Publications, 1991.

24. The journalists, Peter Hounam and Andrew Hogg, produced a book based on their articles: *Secret Cult*, Tring, Herts: Lion, 1984.

25. *ibid* p. 55.

26. Paul Heelas, *The New Age Movement*, Oxford: Blackwell, 1996: III.

27.   See Andrew Rawlinson, 'The Rise and Fall of Lifewave', *Religion Today*, n.d., 4/1-2: 11-14.

28.   See Roy Wallis, 'The Aetherius Society: A Case Study in the Formation of a Mystagogic Congregation', in Roy Wallis (ed.) *Sectarianism: Analyses of Religious Non-Religious Sects*, London: Peter Owen, 1975; Eileen Barker, *New Religious Movements*, London: HMSO 1989: 165-66. The movement's own literature includes a number of books by George King, such as *You Are Responsible!* and (with Kevin Quinn Avery) *The Age of Aetherius*, published by the Society.

29.   See William S. Bainbridge, *Satan's Power: A Deviant Psychotherapy Cult*, Berkeley: University of California Press, 1978, for a monograph about the Process, referred to as the Power by Bainbridge.

30.   See Paul Hawken, *The Magic of Findhorn*, Glasgow: Collins, 1975; Eileen Caddy, *Foundations of Findhorn*, Forres: Findhorn Foundation, 1978; and Carol Riddell, *The Findhorn Community: Creating a Human Identity for the 21st Century*, Forres: Findhorn Press, 1990.

31.   See Vivianne Crowley, *Phoenix from the Flame: Pagan Spirituality in the Western World*, London: Aquarian Press, 1994.

32.   David Burnett, *Dawning of the Pagan Moon: An Investigation into the Rise of Western Paganism*, Eastbourne: March, 1991: 22; 66.

33.   Further information about the range of NRMs in Britain can be gained from several guides, describing or advertising the movements in more or less detail. See, for example, Stephen Annett (ed.) *The Many Ways of Being*, London: Abacus, 1976; Kate Brady and Mike Considine, *The London Guide to Mind Body & Spirit*, London: Brainwave, 1988; Mike Considine, Kate Brady and Marijke Acket, *Survivors London*, London: Alternative Press, 1989; and Robert Adams, *The New Times Network*, London: Routledge, 1982.

34.   Central Office of Information *Britain 1991: An Official Handbook*, London: HMSO, 1991: 239.

35.   Kenneth Robinson, Minister of Health, in the House of Commons, 25 July 1968.

36.   *Enquiry into the Practice and Effects of Scientology*: Report by Sir John G. Foster, KB, QC, MP, December 21, 1971.

37.   After a lengthy appeal, it was agreed she had been wrongfully dismissed, but she did not return to her job with the Council.

38.   For fuller details about these cases and for further discussion concerning NRMs, the State and the legal system in Britain, see Eileen Barker, 'The British Right to Discriminate', in *Society*, 21:4, May-June 1984: 35-41, and in Thomas Robbins and Roland Robertson (eds.) *Church-State Relations: Tensions and Transitions*, New

Brunswick: Transaction, 1986: 329-46; and 'Tolerant Discrimination: Church, State and the New Religions', in Paul Badham (ed.) *Religion, State and Society in Modern Britain*, Lewiston: Edwin Mellen Press, 1989: 185-208.

39. Robert Runcie and George Carey (as Archbishops of Canterbury), successive Moderators of the Free Church Federal Council, and the Roman Catholic Bishop, John Crowley have been Patrons of INFORM. Official representatives of the Church of England, the Roman Catholic and the Free Churches also serve on INFORM's Board of Governors.

40. See *The Cooke Report*, Thames Television, of August 6, 1990.

41. *What is the SAFF?* Leeds, n.d.

42. INFORM is the only organization concerned with NRMs that the British Government has supported. It initially provided 3-year start-up funding, but extended this for a further 3 years (at the rate of £50,000 p.a.) and continues to make extensive use of INFORM's services.

43. Eileen Barker, *New Religious Movements: A Practical Introduction*, London: HMSO, 1989. Italian translation: *I Nuovi Movimento Religiosi: Un' Introduzione Pratica*, Mila: Mondadori, 1992.

44. See James T. Beckford *Cult Controversies* (1985) and Eileen Barker, *New Religious Movements* (1989) for a discussion of potential problems related to some NRMs.

45. The concept of Britian as a gentle secularizing pluralism is expanded in Eileen Barker's 'The Post-War Generation and Established Religion in England', in Jackson Carroll, David Roozen and Wade Clark Roof (eds) *The Baby-Boomers and Mainstream Religion: A Cross-Cultural Study* Boulder, Oxford: Westinton Press 1995: 1-25; see also 'New Lines in the Supra-Market: How much can we buy?' in Ian Hamnett (ed.), *Religious Pluralism and Unbelief: Studies Critical and Comparative*, London: Routledge, 1990: 31-42.

CHAPTER 9

New Religious Movements in the Netherlands

Reender Kranenborg

Multiplicity as basic structure

From the time the Netherlands became independent (1648), diversity of religions has been an accepted fact. In other countries one church or religion usually had official status, and other religions or churches were persecuted, sometimes in a brutal and bloody manner. However, in the Netherlands it has always been different. In the small Dutch republic, consisting of seven states, there was nonetheless one church which had official status: the Calvinistic Reformed Church. It maintained close relations with the authorities and had many privileges.

Nevertheless, other churches and religions could exist in public, with their own buildings and organizations. Notably among these were the Lutheran Church, the Mennonites (Doopsgezinden), the churches of the foreign residence (from England, France, and Armenia) and the Jews (Portuguese and German Jews). However, some churches were forbidden. This did not mean that it was forbidden to confess one's belief or that one had to keep one's membership secret, but it meant that they were not officially allowed to have buildings, or hold open public meetings, etc. Churches in this category were the Roman-Catholics and the 'Remonstranten' (Arminians). Their illegal status, notwithstanding, those churches still erected their own buildings, but they were always hidden behind other buildings, and not clearly visible. Although everyone knew about the existence of these clandestine churches, generally no measures were taken against them. Thus, the Republic of the United Netherlands has always had a variation of faiths and world views. During this period some sects were persecuted, but only if they were very extreme.

During and after the French occupation the separation of church and state was carried out. The Calvinistic Reformed Church

(Nederlandse Hervormde Kerk) lost its privileged position (though some favourable settlements remained) and the other churches gained the freedom to organize themselves according to their own wish. In 1834 a separation took place within the Nederlandse Hervormde Kerk. Orthodox Christians, mostly with a pietistic background, protested against the church, which in their opinion was too liberal and bound too closely to the authorities. At first the protester's right to become a new independent church was denied, but after some struggle with the government they were at last allowed to organize themselves.

Since that time absolute freedom of religion has existed in the Netherlands. It was surprising that many groups split off from this seperated group, in a kind of recurring fraction. The result was, and is, that since that time there have been numerous small independent Reformed churches, sometimes even confined to one town or village. Therefore, in the Netherlands people are used to the existence of many small groups besides the larger established churches and the jewish religion.

As a result of this, in the Netherlands people do not get overly excited when new Christian groups come into existence, which results in a peculiar attitude: often there is a blind eye turned to all that is happening in the area of new Christian groups. We may note that hardly anybody is studying them, and therefore it is very difficult to make an accurate inventory.[1]

Relations Between Church and State

After the French occupation the separation of church and state was accomplished in 1796. After some further regulations and refinements, the law states that the churches are entirely free to organize themselves as they want, and that no church has a privileged position. This separation means that 'The independence of two institutions acknowledging the inevitability of certain mutual bonds'.

The Government does not define the notion of church clearly. The churches are free to define themselves. They determine whether to be a church or not, and the Government has no influence in this matter, unless there are some legal problems involved. This implies that every group or movement which considers itself a church is allowed to do so. Until a few years ago a church had to report itself to the Department of Justice, which entered the name of that group on the list of churches. This registration did not imply any legal recognition or status, and it was therefore impossible to derive legal rights from it.[2] But a group who claims to be a church, of course has certain rights which have been stated in the law, such as the freedom to organize, the freedom of assembly and the exemption from taxation. However, when the government suspects that a certain group is operating under the cloak of a church and making profit, this group can be summoned to appear in court, and in that case the judge has to decide whether this group actually is a church or not. If not, the group is fined, has to pay extra taxes, or may even be outlawed altogether.[3] Recently this registration has been abolished. Groups are no longer required to report to the Department of Justice.[4]

Apart from that, even if a group is entirely free to organize itself, it can be very useful to have a founding statement, clearly formulated aims, a registration of members, statutes, and minutes of the first meeting. For if a group wants to have legal status, it will have to have proper documents. With regard to this legal status, many religious movements have chosen the form of a foundation; in this case one is not free to change the statutes and aims, and the Government has the right to inspect the books, and taxes have to be paid.

It is clear that new religious movements do not have many difficulties in establishing themselves in the Netherlands. It is also clear that it is very difficult to present a survey of all the religious groups in the Netherlands. The most extensive survey (by Hoekstra)[5] lists about 1100 organizations; in fact there may be many more.

The separation between church and state means that no religious organization receives any Government subsidy. They are dependent on the gifts and contributions of members and sympathizers. However, when a religious organization has activities of social or public importance, these activities can be supported by Government subsidy.[6]

Freedom of religion

The Netherlands have absolute freedom of religion. One has the freedom to establish a religion, to have gatherings, to found charitable institutions, to have one's own rituals, to publish, to ask voluntary financial contributions, to have one's own festive days, to raise buildings, to have international contacts, to propagate one's faith, to win new adherents, etc. The government is bound to respect and guarantee this freedom of religion, and when some belief has special requirements, the government has to respect them. If this means that there have to be some exceptional provisions, it is possible to arrange them.[7]

Of course the limit of freedom of religion is determined by the public interest. Not everything is allowed and religious movements also have to respect the law. But it is not clearly defined what is forbidden and in every situation it has to be judged if the limits of public interest are violated. It is thus clear that unlimited freedom does not exist.[8]

In the late 1970's there was a discussion about the dangers of sects to the 'public mental health'. It appeared that the concept 'public mental health' was a difficult one to define and that it was even harder to use it in the daily praxis. Moreover, if a new religious movement can be seen as damaging the public mental health, groups which have existed for many years and which have been accepted, can also be labelled as dangerous to the public mental health. In 1982 it was said that 'New religious movements in general cannot be seen as a danger to the public mental health, but some reactions to it can be seen as such'.[9]

As a result of the massacre at Jonestown, the call for measures against the new religous movements originated. In 1980 the Dutch Parliament installed a committee to investigate the new religious movements and to decide if measures would have to be taken.[10] In 1984 the report was finished with the conclusion that there was no danger to the public mental health and that measures were not necessary. The present legislation is sufficient in case rules are broken.

General survey

As said in the first paragraph, the Netherlands have always known diversity. Here we must note that the Dutch society has never been a whole. Since the last century it has been divided in different segments called 'pillars'. A 'pillar' is a socio-religious group, which comprises all sectors of life. Within the pillar one can find everything one needs: the church (or the party), the school, the university, the trade union, the old people's home, the hospital, the cemetery, the peasant organization, the journal, the broadcasting company, etc.[11] What happened outside their own pillar was known but did not concern those in the group. This implied that other faiths could establish themselves without problems in the Netherlands, as this did not affect the system of the pillars; there was a place for them beside these pillars. People belonging to a particular pillar sometimes looked to the new groups with dismay, and there were theological or ideological reactions, but their right of existence was never discussed. Until the 1960s it was still possible to survey the number of Christian and non-Christian groups. In the case of the Christian groups it was more difficult than in the case of the non-Christian ones, for in the Christian movements the fragmentation was great, but nevertheless it was quite clear which groups existed in the Netherlands of that time.[12]

In the 1960s the situation changed. Dutch society was broken up, the system of the pillars began to shake and many new groups came into existence, especially those groups which presented an alternative to Western society. In this connection the situation in America was important, as the Netherlands had their own protest-movements (Provo) and their own history with psychedelic drugs. So we can see that in the 1960s the religious map of Holland changed enormously. On the one hand we see the emergence of Eastern movements, on the other hand there is a large increase of Christian groups. Existing non-Christian groups also found a new interest among people.

The Movements

In this survey the many New Age groups are not dealt with; this is also the case with the evangelical and pentecostal groups.In the 1960's and also in the 1970's, organized groups arose. Most of them were organized internationally.

The Hare Krishnas arrived in 1970 and had reasonable success until 1979, although the number of their adherents in the Benelux countries have never exceeded one hundred. Recently the very small community has a programme of social welfare for drug addicts and is giving free meals to the homeless in Amsterdam. Some years after the death of Prabhupada, a Dutch member called Hayeshvara Das, came in conflict with the new leaders and founded a new independent group, the 'Shri Chaitanya Gemeenschap'.[13] Transcendental Meditation attracted attention in 1967 and gained much publicity. In the beginning because of the so-called scientific character of the movement, later because of the manifestations of the 'sidhis', and finally because of the idea that TM is very good for physical health. Some years ago TM established in Lelystad a 'sidha-village', based on the 'Maharishi-effect', in order to influence the surroudings and make the town a better and healthier place in which to live. Maharishi himself has his headquarters in the small village of Vlodrop.[14]

The Divine Light Mission (Elan Vital) in the Netherlands had only a short period of activity: in the first half of the 1970s. After the problems between Maharaj Ji with his mother, the movement declined rapidly, and nowadays the question is if they still exist in the Netherlands.

The Bhagwan or Osho movement has been the most spectacular and most frequently discussed movement in the Netherlands. After 1975 the movement began to grow, with spectacular growth in the beginning of the 1980s. Some famous Dutchmen became members, published much about Bhagwan and won many new adherents. In the media the interest was enormous; the movement was discussed vehemently. After Bhagwan left Poona and during his stay in Oregon, the movement diminished, but it still exists and is quite lively. The death of Osho in 1990 has not changed this too much. There are still various centres which are inspired by his ideas; the most important are Osho Humaniversity in Egmond and Osho Supernova in Amsterdam. Many sannyasins use a kind of thera-peutic centre of their own. In New Age groups as 'Avatar' or 'Centre for tantra and intimacy' many of them are active.

Ananda Marga did not play an important role in the Nether-lands. In a part of a province near the German border, a small group came into being, and at one time there was a centre in Amsterdam, but they disappeared long ago. But in 1993 they started a meditation class in Amsterdam again.

The Healthy-Happy-Holy-Organization has existed in the Netherlands since 1970, and have always remained very small; they have courses in kundalini-yoga and a vegetarian restaurant in Amsterdam.

An interesting case is the 'School voor Filosofie', a settlement of the 'School of Economic Science' in London. In 1967 this group came to the Netherlands and began to give courses in practical philosophy (inspired by Vedanta, under influence of the Shankaracharya of Jyotir Math). At the end of the 1970s they attracted many people and began to grow rapidly. In 1983/1984 there was much negative publicity, and the movement changed its tactics. But it still exists and it is still an important and rich movement.

Recently, Sathya Sai Baba is gaining much interest in the Netherlands; many people are travelling to Puttaparthi and back in Holland, forming groups all over the country (there are about 30 small groups now).

As relatively new eastern groups, we will mention the Sahaja Yoga of Mataji (Nirmala Devi) and the Brahma Kumaris. The last one has a course of 'positive thinking' which sometimes is used by the authorities as a part of the educational programme.[15]

We have to remark that in general, yoga is very popular; but mostly the yoga groups do not belong to an Indian organization, and are operating independently. Nevertheless, the religious aspect of it almost always is present.

Here we will mention that in the last ten years the number of the Buddhist groups grew increasingly: we count about 40 groups or centres.[16]

Other new and old movements

Scientology drew the attention of the media in the beginning of the 1970s in a negative way. For about ten years there were difficulties with regard to this movement. After 1984, and especially after the death of Hubbard (1986), the movement became quieter and less aggressive. They did not draw much attention anymore. However, recently (1996) there have again been many problems, resulting in lawsuits and negative publicity.

The Unification Church began as the Unified Family in 1965. In the 1970's there were several problems with parents, mostly in the period between 1978 and 1984. Many of the problems appeared to involve Americans. The number of Dutch people who were associated with the church has always been very small, in total no more than 150 people in the Netherlands. After 1984 the movement declined, and also expressed the wish to have good contacts with the Christian churches.

The Children of God (Family of Love) had a few centres in Amsterdam in the 1970's; they vanished years ago. Occasionally there are rumours that they are existing again under the cover of different names. In 1993 they became active again as 'the Family'.

They have an address in Amsterdam, but they do not have a community in the Netherlands.

Some so-called Christian sects as the Jehovah's Witnesses and the Mormons have existed for a long time in the Netherlands. They have adherents, and slowly are getting more.[17]

Apart from all these groups we see many new evangelical and pentecostal groups. They are fast-growing, and in some places becoming more important than the established churches. In the cities of Amsterdam and Rotterdam the membership of these evangelical groups consist mostly of black people from Africa or Surinam.[18]

Esoteric movements

In the 1980's we see that the esoteric movements, mostly in connection with the New Age, are becoming popular. The two older Theosophical groups, the two Rosicrucian organizations and Anthroposophy enjoy much interest. But there are also new ones. Since 1977 'Mens en Universum' has been active, and also the organization of Benjamin Creme, announcing the coming of Maitreya the Christ. Since 1983 'Psychosofie' exists, a group formed around the medium Zohra (Mme. Bertrand-Noach), who is influenced by the teachings of Alice Bailey. This group has also members which belong to the Christian churches.[19]

New Age

In the period 1978-1984 the growth of the eastern movements stabilized; there are hardly any new adherents. We can also see a shift: people do not join a strongly organized movement, but take a course or some practical lessons within an organization. During that time we saw the growth of the 'spiritual centres' or New Age centres, organizations which offer a variety of courses and lectures, and which function as a kind of community, without strong bonds.[20]

Together with New Age we see Neopaganism; there are some Wicca-groups (Silver Circle), aspects of the 'goddess-movement' and many healing groups.

Since 1984 this trend has continued. The number of eastern groups is not very large, although new ones come into existence regularly. The number of Western esoteric movements is growing strongly, and there is much interest in spiritualism. Since about 1985 this new spirituality has been spoken about in terms of the 'New Age'. Since 1990 the New Age has become very important. There are many groups and organizations; a New Age monthly journal lists about 250 centres and organizations.

Religions of migrants

The new religious movements and the whole of the New Age movement find their adherents almost exclusively among white Dutch people. Nevertheless, we have to state that the total number is not excessively large. In addition to these movements, we find 350,000 Muslims and about 100,000 Hindus in the Netherlands. The Muslims mostly come from Morocco and Turkey and in some cases from Indonesia and Surinam. Their influence in Dutch society is still small and the number of Dutch people who become Muslims is also small (mostly women, married to Muslim husbands). In the Muslim community, especially among those who come from Surinam, the Ahmadiyya-movement (with two organizations) is active, and also is trying to convert Dutch people. Hindus in the Netherlands usually come from Surinam. In the time before the independence of Surinam in 1975, many of them came to the Netherlands. There is hardly any exchange with the Dutch religions: Dutch people do not become Hindu. In the Hindu world in the Netherlands, two organizations are active: the Arya-samaj and the Sanatan Dham (the larger one). The Hare Krishna movement has tried to make contact and work together with these Hindus, but the Hindus did not appreciate the Hare Krishnas and considered them too dogmatic and far too westernized, and the Hare Krishnas had the opinion these Hindus were degenerate and superficial.

In short, the religions of the migrants do not have any influence on the new religious movements or the New Age movement. However, the people from Suriname have imported their own new religious movement, called 'Winti', a kind of spiritualistic healing movement (like 'Candomblé' and 'Umbanda' in South America). We also find Rastafarians among the people who have come from the Dutch Antilles.

Dutch movements

Almost all the new religious movements in the Netherlands have their origins in other countries. They can be found everywhere in the world. Some of the Christian groups in the Netherlands are indigenous, but their number is unknown; in many cases they do not differ very much from other Christian groups, although their organizations are independent and different from one another. In addition we find some exclusive, independent non-Christian groups, mostly confined to one town or village, which will usually disappear when the leader dies. Sometimes a movement is more important: we already mentioned 'Psychosofie', originating in the Netherlands.[21]

Some exclusively independent non-Christian Dutch groups are: the healing movement of the medium Sonja de Vries, the spiritualistic healing movement of the medium Yomanda, the 'Community of God' in Velddriel (possibly not existing any more), the spiritualistic movements 'Harmonia', 'Geesteswetenschappelijk Genootschap De Eeuw van Christus' of Jozef Rulof, and 'Orde der Verdraagzamen', based on the revelations of the medium Karel van der Nagel.

A very special group existed around 'Lou' (Louwrens Voorthuyzen, 1898-1968), who belonged to the ultra-orthodox Reformed churches. He received the revelation that he was God on earth and would not die. After his death the group seemed to dissolve, but recently the older members of the group said they still met together and even had groups in other countries (e.g. in Italy).

Reactions and Approaches

Reactions in the media

At first the press was not very interested in the new religious movements. They were described, and in some extreme cases were discussed, but generally the attitude of the press was positive. Sometimes there was a more extensive article about one of the movements. Only with regard to Scientology were there real problems in the beginning of the 1970s.[22] In 1978 things changed radically. This was caused primarily by the massacre in Guyana. Suddenly many rumours about new religious movements were seen in a different light. After 1978 terrible stories appeared in the papers, and radio and TV gave much negative attention to the sects. The atmosphere inclined towards intolerance. This public feeling reached its peak when in the end of 1983 children were taken away from some of the parents who were members of the Tai-Chi-group in Amsterdam, on the accusation of neglect. This case, which proved to be unjust, enjoyed a great interest in the media. In 1982 P. Schnabel, in charge of the 'Institute of Public Mental Health', published 'Tussen stigma en charisma', which stated there were no real problems with the so-called sects. In 1984 the report of the Parliamentary Committee (author T. Witteveen) was published; again it was shown that there were no real problems with the new religious movements. We can see that after 1984 the public interest in the so-called sects diminished. They were hardly written or spoken about anymore, only in case of extreme situations (as in 1993, caused by the Waco disaster and the Ukrainian Messiah, and in 1994 concerning L. Jouret's Order), but since 1993 the general atmosphere has become negative again.

The parents' associations

In the early days a parents' association did not exist in the Netherlands. Of course, sometimes there were alarmed parents, but this was only incidental and an organization did not come into existence. This situation changed in 1979. The SOS (Samenwerkende Ouders Sekteleden, i.e. parents of children in sects who work together) was founded, as a kind of self-help organization. People, such as parents and relatives of sect members, wanted to have a platform for discussing problems and giving assistance, trying to free the children from the groups in order to give them a better place in society. At the same time they wanted to help the ex-members, and also to generate publicity and to give information at schools about the danger of the new religous movements. Moreover, they wanted the Parliament to investigate the practices of some of the groups; the Parliament installed a committee in 1980. In 1980 the SOS became much more radical, primarily under the influence of the organization of the international parents' associations (at the conference of these organizations in Paris, December 1980) and became an anti-cult movement. It received support from evangelical and right-wing Christian groups, which had strong objections to the Eastern religious movements. They also found support in a television programme, which was very negative about many of the groups. Nevertheless, the SOS has never been very large: about 100 people was the maximum number.[23]

In 1980 two foundations were set up, closely connected with the SOS, with the intention to found a reception centre for ex-members: Joeka and 'Vraag en Aanbod' (Demand and Supply). In 1982 (after a Dutch-German conference in 1981) a centre was founded called 'de Keerkring' (Tropic). The centre did not exist very long: no ex-member was found, so the centre was closed.

The SOS has also thought about the problem of deprogramming. As deprogramming is forbidden by law, the SOS detached itself from it offically. But anyone who wanted to deprogramme his child was sent to an underground organization which did deprogramming. Although there is no precise information, we can state that the number of deprogrammings in the Netherlands has been very low.

After 1984, when the report of the parliamentary committee was published, the SOS lost much of its attraction. The organization existed another seven years, mostly as a self-help group for relatives of sect-members. In 1991 the organization was disbanded.

In 1992 there was word about an unknown anti-cult group, the 'Studie- en hulpgroep sekten' (Organization for study of sects and help of victims). This group had existed since 1984, and has taken over much of the material of the SOS and the 'Nederlandse Vereniging van Ontgoochelden' (see below). The aim is to help people who are inside sects to become conscious of the reasons for their membership. They study the sects by a kind of secret participation in order to get hidden information or documents.

In 1991 a new organization was founded called 'Terug naar af' (Back to the beginning); this organization has as its aim to help people who have problems with Scientology. It ended its activities in 1994.

In 1993 the organization 'Sirenen' (Sirens) was founded. Their aim is to deprogramme people who belong to a 'destructive sect'. As deprogramming is illegal, they have a covert operation. It is not clear how many people are connected with it.

In the 1980s 'Vereniging van Ontgoochelden' (The Dutch Organization of Disappointed People), a group which consisted of ex-members of the Jehovah's Witnesses, and only gave help to members who came out of this group or wanted to come out. In 1987 this anti-cult movement ended its activities as the members joined another religious group 'Eben Haezer'.[24]

Scientific Approaches

In the Netherlands the new religious movements are not studied very much. In the Sociology of Religion the phenomenon of the new religiosity as a cultural fact has been studied, but there has hardly been any interest in specific new religious movements. Only the Free University in Amsterdam has made studies about the new evangelical and pentecostal groups.[25] In the Psychology of Religion department at the Catholic University in Nijmegen, an investigation was made into the motivation of young people who had converted to new religous movements. Research was also done on the question of whether these movements were dangerous to the public mental health. This resulted in a number of different articles, most of them published before 1984.[26]

In the field of the science of religion it was again the Free University which studied the new religious movements. In 1979 a documentation centre was founded (which was closed in 1992) and in 1980 the first issue of the journal 'Religieuze Bewegingen in Nederland' (Religious Movements in the Netherlands) was published.[27]

Reactions from the churches

The churches hardly reacted to the phenomenon of the new religious movements. The largest Reformed Church (Nederlandse Hervormde Kerk) edited a pastoral letter in 1982, the first and the last thing which has been done on this subject in this church. The second largest Reformed Church (Gereformeerde Kerken in Nederland) established a small committee in 1978 in order to supply material for information and discussion about the new religiosity.[28] The Dutch Roman Catholic Church translated the official report of the Vatican in 1986, without a comment.

The Dutch Council of Churches was more active. This Council has a section for Interreligious Encounter, with a subsection for new religiosity. This subsection is a continuation of the committee of the Gereformeerde Kerken in Nederland (mentioned above). This subsection responds to requests of new religious movements and produces materials for discussion and information. Thus, a booklet was published about new spiritual movements and in 1993 a book about New Age. Booklets about Hinduism, Islam and Buddhism in the Netherlands were published. It was this section which urged the Dutch Council of Churches to react strongly against the proposal of Cottrell in the European Parliament in Strassburg, in 1983/84. Because of this section the World Council of Churches convened a meeting on the new religious movements which was held in Amsterdam in 1986.

In the churches members react quite differently. In the right-wing orthodox groups the dangers and seductions of eastern groups and occultism are vehemently warned against. In the period of 1978-1984 this critical trend merged together with the general negative mood against new religious movements. After 1984 this wing has displayed much criticism against the New Age movement, strongly inspired by American fundamentalist groups.

On the other hand, there are Christians within the churches who have a more positive attitude towards the new religiosity. In the Catholic Church there are various monasteries where monks use yoga and zen techniques, and repeat the mantra OM.[29]

In the Protestant churches this is different; people sometimes like to discuss the new ideas and try to integrate them in their belief system.

Conclusions

The new religious movements in the Netherlands have never been a big problem. There has also never been a real anti-cult movement.

To new religious movements the Netherlands is a country without many problems; there was freedom and it was possible to do everything one wanted, only general laws must not be broken.

Although the field of the new religious movements is very broad (there are hundreds of groups) the number of people involved was not very large. But we can see that many ideas of the new religiosity are influential among other people, who try to combine them with their own particular world view.

The number of well organized movements has diminished, but the number of loosely organized movements or organizations is still growing.

We can see the importance of the phenomenon of spiritual centres increasing.

At first there was a great interest in the Eastern movements. Later on the interest in Western-esoteric groups and old non-Christian groups increased and surpassed the interest in the Eastern groups.

We now see that all is merging into the New Age Movement.

Notes

1. Recently H.C. Stoffels has studied these Christian Reformed groups and published a survey; the results were printed in *Religieuze Bewegingen in Nederland* 26 (1993).

2. The Church of Scientology tried to do this. It claimed to be an official church, as it was registered on the official list.

3. The 'Satanskerk' (Church of Satan) in Amsterdam is the best known example of an organization which claimed to be a church and was declared by the judge not to be a church. In fact it was a sex club in the red light district in Amsterdam; the connected 'Order of the Walburgians' consisted of prostitutes. This Church of Satan had no relations with the international Church of Satan in San Francisco.

4. In 1982, 277 groups (or churches) had been registered since the beginning in 1853. Most registrations dated from the 1970s. The list was never controlled; consequently, the list contains names of groups which do not exist anymore.

5. In his encyclopedia of religion in the Netherlands, *Wegwijs in Religieus en Levens beschouwelijk Nederland*, 1995, second edition.

6. Thus, the churches receive subsidies for their youth work, the old peoples homes, social and welfare work, etc. As far as I know only one of the religious movements, TM, had temporarily received financial support from the local authorities for some of their activities. Scientology tried to get a subsidy for Narconon, but as far as I know the group did not receive it.

7. For instance the ritual slaughtering by Jews and Muslims, or the cremation by Hindus. Here dispensations can be given. On the other hand the government cannot use compulsion: when people refuse vaccination on religious grounds, the authorities cannot compel people to be vaccinated. From time to time there is a discussion about this, when as a result of non-vaccination, an illness will become epidemic; in 1992 this was the case in the Dutch 'bible belt', when polio became epidemic in a certain area.

8. Financial manipulation is not allowed, rebellion against the authorities is forbidden, the public order may not be disturbed, and it is of course forbidden to kidnap people, etc. Until now only in a few cases have problems arisen.

9. Some people consider, for instance, the Unification Church a danger to the public mental health, because it is said this church puts pressure on the members, alienates them from their parents and family, brainwashes them, and refuses to let people go. But some of these points can also be said of some of the very small reformed churches: there is a strong pressure on the members, people are taught that they will surely go to hell if they break with the group, and some normal activities such as watching television and some medical treatments are forbidden. The quotation is from P. Schnabel.

10. The Divine Light Mission, the Bhagwan movement, the Hare Krishnas, Transcendental Meditation, Scientology, Unification Church and the (very unknown) Jesus-children were investigated.

11. The largest pillars were those of the protestants, the catholics, the socialists and the liberals.

12. Among the Christian groups listed are: Methodism, Pietism, Adventism, Maranatha-movement (a Dutch group), three Apostolic churches, Baptism, the movement of the Möttlingers, Church of the Brethern, Buchman movement, Moral Rearmament, Salvation Army, Old Catholics, Oxford Catholic movement, Pentecostals, Darbism, Quakers, 'Stromen van kracht'. Among the non-Christian movements: Christian Science, Bahai, Sufi-movement, Theosophy, Anthroposophy, Community of Christians (*Christengemeinschaft*), astrology, Bellamy-movement, Mazdaznan, Freemasons, Odd Fellows, spiritualism, Rosicrucians (AMORC and Lectorium Rosicrucianum), Mormons, Reorganised Mormons, Theocratical State of Sion, Foursquare Gospel, Jehovah's Witnesses, New World Servants, 'Tempelbouwers' (a Dutch esoteric group), 'Neoreligie' (a Dutch liberal humanistic religion), Lou-movement (around a Dutch manifestation of God), Liberal Catholics, Swedenborgians, Krishnamurti.

13. As far as I know it has only one centre, in Amsterdam.

14. It is interesting that some health insurance companies give a reduction to people who are doing meditation in the TM-organization. Some car insurance companies do the same. Someone has convinced them that practising TM means one will be healthier and quieter: therefore less accidents are likely to take place. If this is really the case, and remains the case, is a question. The siddha-village in Lelystad until now has not proved that the situation in this town has improved much. At present TM is propagating Ayurveda medicine in an academy of its own.

15.   There are more eastern movements, e.g. the group of Babaji (of Herakhan), Eckankar, Radha Soami Satsang, Ramakrishna movement, Divine Life Society, Siddha-yoga of Muktananda, Ram Chandra Mission, Sri Chinmoy movement, Ammachi-movement, Self-Realization Fellowship, Kriya Yoga, Aurobindo Movement, Satyam Shivam Sundaram, the group of Yogeshvarananda, Followers of Krishnamurti, Vimala Thakar and U.G., and Brahma Rishi Movement. Some further information: in 1982 we can find the following figures of membership: Radha Soami Satsang 400, Yoga and Vedanta 5000, Eckankar 150 interested people, Sidhhayoga 150 interested people, Babaji centre about 100 visitors, Kriya-yoga 200 interested people.

16.   The most important are 'Boeddhistische Unie van Nederland', 'Stichting vrienden van het Boeddhisme', 'Friends of the Westen Buddhist Order', 'Nederlands Boeddhistisch Studiecentrum', Boeddharama, Buddhavihara, Dhammavihari, 'Nederlandse Buddha-Dhamma Stichting', Sayagi U Ba Khin stichting, Arya Maitreya Mandala, Dharmadhatu, Döphan-Ling, Stichting Dzogchen, Karma Deleg Chö Phel Ling, Maitreya-instituut, Nyingma Centrum, Rigpa, Sakya Thegchen Ling Boeddhistisch Centrum, and some zen-groups.

17.   Some other groups: The Real Truth (World Wide Church of God), Unity Nederland.

18.   It is not possible to give a survey of all these groups. It is very difficult because they mostly operate on their own; every group is independent.In a new part of Amsterdam ('Bÿlmermeer'), we count more than 40 independent churches.

19.   We can also mention Agni-yoga, Church Universal and Triumphant (Summit Lighthouse), Martinus-groups, Bô Yin Râ, Gurdjieff-groups, followers of Stephan Lubienski, the Sufi-Movement, Subud, adherents of Jakob Lorber, Sivas, New Theosophical Union, and Kabalistic groups.

20.   The first of these centres, founded in 1969 in Amsterdam, was the international famous 'De Kosmos'; it closed the doors in 1992, for the competition of the many new centres everywhere in the country was too strong.

21.   More information can be found in the paper delivered at the CESNUR-conference in Foggia, Sept. 1989 by R. Kranenborg (published in 1991 in *Le Nuova Rivelazione*; an English version appeared in 1993 in *SYZYGY* 2/1.2).

22.   In 1972 a journalist, at the request of the Department of Justice, made an investigation into the practices of Scientology. After publishing his results (in a journal), Scientology protested sharply.

According to some of his colleagues, this caused the journalist's death after he had suffered a heart attack. The investigation was ended, but renewed by a parliamentary committee in 1980.

23. In 1982 SOS received 56 requests for help, and 120 requests for information. In that year the SOS had 43 occasions to give information at schools, and distributed around 300 booklets. 11 ex-members were also helped.

24. The Dutch branch of the evangelical 'Greek concordant text' group, founded by Adolph Ernst Knoch (1874-1965).

25. See the studies from H.Stoffels, who published two special issues of the Journal 'Religieuze Bewegingen in Nederland' (Religious Movements in the Netherlands) about evangelicals and pentecostals (1984 and 1990). In 1990 he wrote his thesis about the Dutch evangelicals. He also published a book about the so called 'growth-movements' (Gestalt, est, psychosynthesis, Gurdjieff groups, Aurobindo yoga, TM, Bhagwan). In 1991 S.J. Vellinga also wrote a thesis about the Dutch evangelicals and pentecostals.

26. We can mention the publication of J.v.d.Lans' *Volgelingen van de goeroe* (Followers of the guru). In the journal "Religieuze Bewegingen in Nederland" various articles were published (about deprogramming, the situation of ex-members, conversion, the problems with the Tai-chi group, and the mental health of members of groups). After 1985 this department did not study the groups further.

27. In 1974 the thesis of R. Kranenborg was published about certain religious movements *Zelfverwerkelijking* ('Self-realisation'). The first book about this theme in the Netherlands. Research was done on the psychedelic religion of Leary, yoga, 3HO, Macrobiotics, TM, and Hare Krishna. In 1977 he published on Transcendental Meditation. In 1979 he became the founder of the documentation centre at the Free University and in 1980 of the journal 'Religieuze Bewegingen in Nederland'. In 1982 a study followed about certain groups (four yoga groups, Divine Light Mission, Bhagwan movement, Unification Church, Hare Krishna, Transcendental Meditation). In 1984 he published 'Een nieuw licht op de kerk?' (A New Light on the Church?) This book deals with general questions about the so-called sects and discusses theological implications. In 1988 a collection of texts of Hindu-gurus was published; in 1988 and in 1989 two books about reincarnation were also written by him. In 1994 a book was published about New Age ('De andere weg van Jezus').The Journal 'Religieuze Bewegingen in Nederland' has two issues every year (each containing about 125 pages). The intention is to describe movements as well as possible. They are mostly special issues. Until now 32 issues have been published.

28.   Some booklets about Hinduism, Islam, Bhagwan, TM and the Unification Church were produced.

29.   For instance, the Jesuit Karel Douven, who invented a complete 'New Age theology', and founded a group, together with the Protestant theologian Klink, in order to combine esoteric ideas with the Christian creed. Furthermore the former Jesuit Bernard Huybers, famous composer of church hymns, is now an important New Age speaker.

CHAPTER 10

New Religious Movements in Germany

Thomas Gandow

New Religious Movements and the 'Youth Religions'

Today the term *'Neue religiöse Bewegungen'* ('New Religious Movements') is usually much more understood in Germany to mean the Taize young people, the groups around charismatic revivalists, parts of the New Age trend, spiritual trends within the women's movement, etc.

There have been various suggestions for using other terms for the groups and trends which are included in the English usage of the term 'New Religious Movements'.

One thing that was important for the German usage was the observation that these groupings are not so much trends and milieus, but rather are very structured organizations. It was also noted that based neither on their own self-understanding nor on their history and structure could they be considered sect-like groups that have split off from main organizations or religions, but rather they are organizations which claim originality.The new Japanese groups have also long been called 'New Religions' in German.

In Germany the term 'Youth Religions' as used by F.W. Haack and others, has become common for these groups. For one thing, it designates concrete organizations and groups and not only milieus or trends, and for another, it avoids from the outset judgmental terms such as 'controversial new religious movements' or even 'youth sects'.[1]

The usage of the term 'New Religious Movements' will not be further discussed here. The usage of this term has not become common in Germany, or more precisely, it is used for something completely different from the English term.

When in the following report I discuss the subject of 'New Religious Movements', I will attempt where possible to use terms which, in my opinion, are more appropriate.

New Religious Movements and Organizations in Germany: The Present Situation[2]

Movements which very early introduced new religious trends from oriental and occult backgrounds

It is certainly not necessary to report here on the Anthroposophical Society of Rudolf Steiner which arose from the Theosophical movement in Germany. Compared with the influence of the Anthroposophical Society and its branches in religious, pedagogical, economic and medical areas, other theosophical groups in Germany have hardly played a role until the appearance of the New Age movement. Other notable groups in this area are the OTO (Ordo Templi Orientis) as well as various Rosicrucian groups and the Grail movement.

Religious movements and organizations with 'German' background

Neo-Germanic and 'folk-religious' (völkisch religiöse) groups:

A special role is played even today by small 'folk-religious' groups. Some of them supposedly are based on heathen roots and traditions in the broadest sense, whereby 'Celtic' and 'Slavic' elements are incorporated along with the 'Germanic.' There are also clearly racist-religious groups which claim 'through blood' to be the inherited and revealed religion of the Teutons as the forefathers of the Germans. It is often discussed whether the Hitler Movement of National Socialism wasn't itself a kind of religious movement.

New Christian sects from Germany:

Some of the new Christian sects such as the New Apostolic Church, the Apostolate Jesu Christi and the Apostolate of Juda began in Germany or exist only in Germany. The spiritist 'Johannische Kirche' of Berlin can also be mentioned in this group.

Esoteric and neognostic ideologies and systems from Germany:

The Anthroposophical Society and its diverse branches was mentioned above. It is one of the largest of the new religious groups with a large influence beyond Germany. Its forms have already overcome many interdisciplinary as well as national borders. It ranges from its own educational system (Waldorf Schools) to biological-dynamic agriculture, a 'holistic' art form, and the 'anthroposophically extended' medicine to an anthroposophically inspired and initiated Christian sect (denomination), 'The Christian Community'/Christengemeinschaft.

The Grail movement with its international influence must at least be mentioned here. The most important 'native' new religion is 'Universal Life' which has recently been very effective. Univeral Life is a new-revelation religion based around Gabriele Wittek of Wurzburg. She is considered a prophet and possibly also the reincarnation of the repentant 'Satana'. The group around Frau Wittek was originally more eschatologically oriented and called itself the 'Heimholungswerk Jesu Christi'.

'Brothers from the semi-material world' were to pick up the members out of this world, among other means, through UFO's. The concept from Christian-spiritist tradition has been more and more influenced by Asian religiosity. Prof. Hofmann, one of the most important inspirers of Frau Witteck, is a former TM teacher. Today, however, Frau Witteck wants to stay on this earth, or more exactly, she wants to build a 'Christ-state' with the centre in Würzburg am Main. It should cover all areas of human life. A development with numerous practical initiatives for life reforms, comparable to the practical concrete forms of anthroposophy, seems feasible.

Which groups are the most important ones?

Islam:

Though not usually considered a 'new religious group', the various movements and groups within the Muslim context can be included, as today they are important not only for foreign workers and immigrants, but also have more and more influence on interested Germans. The importance, and the publicity work, especially of the missionary groups — various Sufi groups, the Ahmadyya movements, and not least the Baha'i movement, emanating from Islam but persecuted by Muslims — is increasing and is not limited to subculture groups only.

'Buddhist' groups:

The various Buddhist groups have certainly become culturally important among the new religious movements. The groups are probably the same ones as in other European countries.

An increase is probably also seen in the Japanese new religions (especially Soka Gakkai) which present themselves as 'Buddhist', but also various Japanese Ki groups.

New Christian groups:

In the Christian area, especially those charismatic, neo- pentecostal and fundamentalist groups which are influenced in Germany and Europe by groups from the USA, should be noted. In addition to founding their own new groups, they have also been influential through a great number of newly established native groups which have started as a reaction to them, both in imitation and in rejection of them.

Youth Religions and Psycho-groups:

An especially important role is played in Germany by those groups called 'Youth Religions', rigidly structured new religious groups and guru movements
- because of their influence on youth and social subcultures (for example ISKCON)
- but also because of their intensive activities (for example Scientology,[3] and Moon movement).[4]
- in the health field (Transcendental Meditation)
- in politics (for example Transcendental Meditation, Scientology[3] and especially the Moon movement). [5]

Controversies

There are probably controversies surrounding every active religious group. The decision in favour of a group or the recruitment into a religious group can create controversy at least in the area of the family and profession. It is surprising that public activities such as fundraising, PR activities etc., but also the successful advertising work of most of the religious groups, doesn't cause much controversy probably because of the transparency and extensive information available.

However there can be social controversies which arise around a certain group or perhaps are even created specifically by the group itself.

Many controversies surrounding new religious groups can arise and be explained through difficulties in acculturation. Therefore one shouldn't be surprised when such controversies are especially common with regard to groups from foreign cultural backgrounds. However, it does seem that certain dishonest advertising and fundraising methods are the cause of more problems and controversies than cultural differences.

Especially those groups who present themselves as 'Western' or 'American' seem to mobilize a particularly high potential of controversy.

Among the guru movements there is the strongly 'American' oriented TM movement.[6] Otherwise most conflicts seem to be around the Moon movement, Scientology, and the so-called Boston Church of Christ.

A deliberate instigation of controversy is brought about by the Moon movement as a regular part of their missionary and PR activity.

There have also been controversies regarding the work of Youth Religions in the 'new German states' (the former East Germany). It was again made clear that the main reason for the development of problems, controversies, and criticism lies in the hidden, false representations, and deceptive methods of the groups. The greatest controversies at the present time in Germany certainly arise from the Scientology organization. The opinion of the Federal Government is:

that the Scientology sect is neither a religious community nor a world view organization, and that it thus cannot claim Article 4, Paragraph 1 and 2 of the Basic Law in connection with Article 137 WRV (Weimar Reich Constitution). (Statement of the Federal Ministry for Youth, Family and Women from October 23rd, 1990).

Because of the considerable criticism and objections to its economic activities, Scientology has partly begun to register the economic activities of its course sales as a business enterprise. At the same time, the organization tries to present itself as a persecuted religious minority in Germany.

In this regard, Scientology began a 'Call to Arms Germany' campaign on May 4th, 1994 and founded a 'Germany Task Force' I/OSA INT 'to defend itself against supposed neo-nazi government attacks on the Scientology organization and members in Germany'.

The conference of German interior ministers stated in a press release on May 6th, 1994 regarding 'observations of the Scientology Organization':

The interior ministers are of the opinion that the state of knowledge at present does not allow the nationwide classification into the category of political endeavors. At the present time, the Scientology Organization represents to the authorities responsible for the defence of danger and for criminal prosecution an organization which, under the guise of a religious community, combines elements of economic crimes and psycho-terror towards its members with economic activity and a sectarian approach. The focal point of its activities seems to be in the area of economic crimes. Therefore, state defensive measures should first be continued in this area.

Numbers[7]

It is difficult to make concrete statements about membership numbers. For some groups, for example the Moon movement, their appearance and presence in Germany has now been transferred to Eastern Europe.

Local chapters of the Moon Movement in various German cities were closed in the last years. Nevertheless there were still about 200 nucleus members and more than 2,000 employees in the machine construction factory which belongs to the Moon movement.

On the other hand influence can be measured which is based on concepts such as karma and reincarnation. Polls have been taken in this area. In an article on March 1st, 1993 the *Frankfurter Allgemeine* reported that already 12% of German citizens over 16 believed in reincarnation. 14% were undecided. The newspaper quotes the Allensbacher Polling Institute with the statement:

only 74% completely rejected the belief in this concept of the soul and rebirth which actually belongs to the Hindu-Buddhist understanding of religion and is actually alien to the Christian-Western world.

Especially young people with above-average levels of education looked for spiritual experiences in this reincarnation belief, while the older generations were more cautious because the institute supposed that as children and young people they had been exposed in a very definite way to the Christian concepts of eternal life. The Allensbach researchers commented with astonishment on the increase in these numbers:

The belief in the transmigration of souls used to be limited in our cultural area primarily to a relatively small circle of Theosophists and Anthroposophists.

Researching the NRM scene

In Germany there has been a long tradition for not only *academic* but also *critical* study of the 'New Religious Movements', including Asian groups, with Europe as their mission field, as well as Youth Religions, etc. The research, discussions, and academic reports, have been particularly in the field of missionary studies, as is probably the case in other European countries too. The first thorough studies were published in the mission-study journals and publications. Even non-church oriented writers can, and do, have their studies published there.

It would be worthwhile to quote here some of the older, partially quite detailed essays, monographs, articles and collections of articles and essays, especially if one also considers the publications before the Second World War as well as English articles by German writers from the IRE. A history of the research has not been published and this isn't the place to do that. Readers who are interested can find helpful information in R. Hummel: *Indische Mission und neue Frömmigkeit im Westen — Religiöse Bewegungen Indiens in westlichen Kulturen*, Stuttgart 1980, particularly in the extensive notes.

Churches

In addition to the above studies, there are also in Germany professionally and academically qualified church-related structures and persons who study the new religious organizations and problems arising from them.

One can say that the church's concern with the 'newcomers' is not just a 'reaction' but from the beginning the church has (of course critically) followed the development. Almost all the new religious groups from the beginning of their appearance in Germany, and German-speaking countries, have been academically and critically documented and have for the most part been included from the beginning in a critical dialogue with church specialists, reseachers and consultants.

How did it happen that there has been such an intensive church-sponsored concern and activity in regard to issues of sects and ideologies?

Professional church interest in issues of sects and ideologies in Germany partly goes back to, and is rooted in, the theological-academic and aggressive clashes of the church with the ideology of National Socialism. Because of these roots in the 'Kirchenkampf' of the Evangelical Church in the Nazi era, the 'Materialdienst der EZW', the journal of the EKD's (Evangelical Church in Germany) institution, the 'Evangelical Central Office for Issues of Ideologies' in Stuttgart which was founded in 1960, proudly called 1994 the 57th year of its publication.

EZW:

The Evangelische Zentralstelle für Weltanschauungsfragen (EZW), Evangelical Central Office for Issues of Ideologies, in Stuttgart was founded by Pastor Kurt Hutten, who consciously continued the work of the 'Apologetics Centre' in Berlin which had been closed by the Gestapo.

As an institution of the EKD, the EZW was officially established in 1960 as a church-sponsored, but independently organized, institution directed by a board of trustees. Academic specialists from various areas and focal points work in the EZW according to their qualifications as sociologists, specialists in mission and religious studies , theologians, etc. At the present time (1997), there are five academic staff members in the office in Berlin.

Seers, Brooders, and Enthusiasts:

A well-known and basic work for church and academic studies on issues of sects and ideologies as well as new religious groups was K. Hutten's book *Seher, Grübler, Enthusiasten — Sekten und religiöse Sondergemeinschaften der Gegenwart*[8] which was published from 1950 to 1968 in 11 printings with over 50,000 copies. In addition to descriptions of the classical and new Christian sects (including Pentecostal and Faith Healing movements) it presented in the edition from 1968 comprehensive articles and information on the origin, doctrine and background of more than 15 additional new religious groups and organizations. In order to document the range of the work in regard to 'non-classical organizations, here are some of the 'newer' groups which are considered in the book: 'Baha'i-Religion'; 'Bund der Kämpfer für Glaube und Wahrheit' (Horpeniten); 'Eglise Chretienne Universelle' (Georges Roux); 'Evangelisch-Johannische Kirche'; 'Gemeinschaft in Christo Jesu' (Lorenzianer), 'Gottesbund (Loge) Tanatra'; 'Gralsbewegung'; 'International New Thought Alliance'; 'Lorbeerbewegung'; 'Lou-Gruppe'; 'Mazdaznan-Bewegung'; 'Neue Kirche'; 'Neugeist Bund'; 'Peace Mission' (Father Divine); 'Unity, School of Christianity'.

A twelfth edition of the book was published in 1982 in a completely revised and greatly expanded version (still in print). It was revised and completed by H.D. Reimer and concentrates mostly on Christian groups. Therefore the Moon movement, for example, which was formerly called the 'Society for the Unification of World Christianity', is no longer included. On the other hand, Mormons and Baha'i continue to be presented; there is also a comprehensive chapter on the UFO movement in relation to the account of spiritist groups.

Materialdienst der EZW

Since 1960 the journal of the EZW, the 'Materialdienst der EZW' has appeared which was first published again by K. Hutten since the end of the 1940s. Today it is a monthly journal on ideologies, sects, new religious groups and religions. In addition to basic articles and research reports, there are occasionally reports from representatives of new religious groups and documented self-presentations.

Besides the regular publication of the journal, there are other publications by the EZW which among other topics also include aspects of the new religious groups.

Arbeitskreis Religiöse Gemeinschaften der VELKD:

The Arbeiskreis Religiöse Gemeinschaften der Vereinigten Evangelisch-Lutherischen Kirche in Deutschland (Committee for Religious Communities of the United Evangelical-Lutheran Church in Germany) — VELKD, is a group of experts in religious studies, as well as theologians and researchers who were appointed by VELKD. Included are 'commissioners' and university teachers. This study group writes the *Handbuch Religiöse Gemeinschaften*.[9]

Handbuch Religiöse Gemeinschaften
(Handbook of Religious Communities)

This handbook was first developed in 1952 as an attempt, following the Second World War, to create a church information booklet explaining the position of religious restructuring and orientation as a consequence of war and refugee situations. It should address questions of church membership as well as possibilities for cooperation. It was first published in 1966 in the form of a loose-leaf collection of information, and in 1978 the Handbook was published for the first time as a book, which is still available in bookshops.

Already at that time, in addition to free churches — special Christian fellowships and Christian sects, new 'world views' such as theosophy, anthroposophy, Rosicrucians, Welt-Spirale, Spiritism, Transcendental Meditation (TM) were represented. 'New Religions (Youth Religions) in Europe' were: 'Hare Krishna', 'Unification Church', 'Scientology Church of Germany', 'Children of God'.
The Handbook was published in 1994 in a fourth edition.

On the one hand it is considered the standard work which describes the religious groups; their origins and history, a summary of their doctrines or ideologies, working methods, and organizational structure, cultic meetings and activities. Sources and literature are presented thoroughly, partly using the documents of the respective organizations.

On the other hand, the book also includes a separate section in which there is an evaluation from the Protestant/Lutheran point of view with regard to each group, as well as suggestions for practical behavior in response to the various groups or movements as a whole, but also towards the individual members.

In this way, the following new religious groups, organizations, and trends, as well as churches, free churches and Christian sects, are thoroughly described (1994).

Aktionsanalytische Organization (AAO)/Friedrichshof-SD-
Movement/Muehl Movement
Ahmadiyya
Ananda Marga
Anthroposophy
Bhagwan-Rajneesh-Movement/Rajneesh Foundation
International/Osho-Commune
Baha'i
Brahma Kumaris
Buddhist Context: Vipassana; Kagyüdpa
Centre for Experimental Forming of Society (Zentrum für
Experimentelle Gesellschaftsgestaltung ZEGG) Projekt
Meiga/Duhm-Movement
Children of God (CoG) Family of Love
Church of Jesus Christ of Latter Day Saints/Mormons
EST/Forum/Centres Network
Germanic-Believers and Folk-Religious groups
Grailmovement
Hindu Context: Guruism; Yoga; Tantrism; Reincarnation
International Society for Krishna Consciousness (ISKCON)
Japanese Context: Ki-Groups; Nichiren Soshu; Soka Gakkai
Moon Movement
New Age
New Witches
Rosicrucians
Sathya Sai Baba and his Movement
Shiite Context: Ahmadiyya; Baha'i
Scientology/Dianetics
Spiritism
Sri Chinmoy and the Sri Chinmoy Centres
Subud
Theosophy
Transcendental Meditation (TM)

Umbanda
Universal Life/Heimholungswerk Jesu Christi (UL/HHW)

Commissioners from the Regional Churches:

Since the middle of the 1960s all the regional church offices of the Evangelical Church in Germany have gradually appointed 'Commissioners for Issues of Sects and Ideologies' — at first as voluntary or part-time staff workers. These church commissioners, are mostly pastors, and as such, theologians specializing in religious studies, mission theology, sociology of religion or pastoral psychology, but specialists in religious education are also included. These respective commissioners deal with all matters which concern sects, ideologies and religions, especially research and information, but also advising and pastoral counselling.

Friedrich-Wilhelm Haack, the Commissioner of the Evangelical Lutheran Church of Bavaria, has especially influenced the profile of the work of these church commissioners for sects and ideologies. The results of his research, gained through research work in Germany and on trips throughout the world, many together with Dr Rüdiger Hauth — especially to India, East Asia and the two American continents, have been presented for discussion in a great number of publications. Typical for Haack's and Hauth's style and methods (and thus influential to a whole generation of church specialists and researchers in Germany), is the 'nearness', investigative, field-work and encounters of the direct dialogue with members, leaders and gurus of the new religious groups, sects, circles, orders, etc.

Munich Series and other publications:

Many of the research reports and monographies of the 'Regional Church Commissioners' and other specialists have been published in the 'Münchener Reihe', a series of paperback books founded by F.W. Haack. Each year, up to six new books and collections of material regarding questions of sects and ideologies are published — also in the field of youth religions, the new religious organizations, and the occult. These reports are often first-time presentations, not only for the German-speaking world. One can mention in particular the publications on TM, Scientology, Moon

Movement, Mormons, Satanism, New-Revelation Movements, etc. There is also a magazine *Berliner Dialog*, published in Denmark and printed in the German language. (See Chapter 12, End Note 1).

Catholic Church:

The Roman Catholic dioceses in Germany, Austria and Switzerland have also now appointed 'commissioners', who work in a similar manner to their Protestant colleagues. One of the products of the work of the Roman Catholic commissioners is a dictionary of sects, special groups, and ideologies.[10] This dictionary of 'Religious Groups and Terms' is now available in paperback form, and contains encounters and discussions with these groups. The writers of the individual articles are Protestant and Catholic specialists for sect issues, primarily from Germany, Austria and Switzerland.

Non-Church Research

Religious Studies, Universities:

Specialists from the fields of the history of religion, religious studies, and the sociology of religion have of course also been involved in the study of the new religious groups and movements.[11]

After the appearance of publicly acknowledged problems with youth religions and similar groups in Germany, the Federal Government appointed various experts, especially sociologists of religion and psychologists, to study youth religions, and made considerable sums of money available for this research. (Probably more than DM 300,000 for the so-called Viennese Study alone). Unfortunately, many of the studies remained unsatisfactory because of insufficient use of sources, and methodological problems, not only in light of the evaluations. Also the academic discussion regarding these studies never really got started, probably because of the inadequacies mentioned above.

Even those writers who sometimes strongly criticize the positions and understandings of the church commissioners and the Evangelical Central Office for Issues of World Views, publish their studies in church publications and are hardly discussed. The obvious inability to instigate a serious discussion with new points of view and individual research results, led some writers to considerable bitterness, especially towards the seemingly more 'successful' church related authors. These church related writers are said to have 'stigmatized' not only the 'new religious movements' but also the 'secular' academics who supposedly approached the topics 'without prejudice'. On the one hand, a completely exaggerated picture of the possibilities of church relations work is drawn. On the other hand, the fact is covered up that some of the so-called 'scientific' and independent researchers (including of course also theologians!) have become regular advocates of youth religions and other new religious movements and regular attenders at their conferences.

Religious studies are not only taught in Marburg in Germany. There are a number of universities, including the Free University of Berlin, where objective work is done in regard to the 'New Religious Movements'.

Student Initiatives:

The new religious trends have also led to a growing interest in religious studies and the history of religion. Many of the active students and young graduate students and doctoral candidates have tried to deal with their own youth experiences through their university studies. Similar situations can also be seen in other subject areas.

Parent Initiatives:

There are two roots for the parent initiatives in Germany: One important impulse came from the work of church-sponsored pastoral work and counselling. The initiatives with the largest number of members are those which were based on the church work of the commissioners for issues of sects and ideologies in Munich, Berlin and Nordelbien, as well as Hannover. They all have supraregional importance and membership. In addition to these there are smaller 'parent initiatives' in various parts of Germany, some of them influenced by foreign impulses. Most of the initiatives however work on a voluntary basis and are mainly concerned with individual and social effects of belonging to a sect, youth religion, or psycho-cult. The ideological background and working methods of the 'parent initiatives' can vary greatly.

Kidnapping/deprogramming:

In Germany there is no kidnapping/deprogramming taking place in the field of new religious groups. All the relevant parent initiatives have followed the example of the Munich parent initiative and have credibly distanced themselves at an early stage from such methods. The Berlin Parent and Concerned Persons Initiative made the following statement on November 14th, 1982:

The membership of the Parent Initiative against Psychic Dependency and Religious Extremism Berlin e.V. (today: Parent and Concerned Persons Initiative against Psychic Dependency for Mental Freedom Berlin e.V. (EBI) in light of the press reports and questions from its members, as well as deprogramming offers made to the association, has on Nov 14th, 1982 discussed the 'Munich Statement' and unanimously accepted it and has since then strengthened its content in various ways. It is still definitive today for the Eltern and Concerned Persons Initiative against Psychic Dependency for Mental Freedom Berlin e.V.

The Parent and Concerned Persons Initiative against Psychic Dependency for Mental Freedom e.V. rejects without compromise the so-called deprogramming which is based on the denial of freedom and uses mental or external pressure. It warns all parents against putting their children through such a procedure. Professional deprogrammers who offer their services should be turned away immediately and the incident should be reported to the EBI. The EBI warns against subjecting youth to such a procedure which is equivalent to brain-washing. The EBI also notes that one of the consequences can be an even stronger tie to the youth religion or sect out of which one was trying to rescue the person. When illegal procedures are used one must also reckon with considerable legal consequences (in the area of civil law as well as criminal law) which will confront the parents or the family member who instigated the deprogramming.

At the same time the EBI thoroughly rejects all attempts to defame and decry those family members who in their emergency situation see no other possible way out than deprogramming. Misguided by fear about their child or partner and through bad advice, they have taken upon themselves great pangs of conscience and extensive expenses and efforts in order to help their child or family member. Great fear, and a small hope, have led them to take that step. Only the legal institutions can judge them.

In any case, the sects and youth religions should not judge these methods, as they themselves use a dangerous form of deprogramming and brainwashing through their missionary programmes, thereby, to a large extent, creating the basis for the parents and family members actions.

Groups which injure the right of the individual to true religious freedom by their indoctrination methods have no right to act as if they were the guardians of religious freedom. However the EBI points out again that the unjust actions of the youth religions and sects does not justify using unjust measures in confronting them. Only decisive and clear information carries a chance of having a long term effect on curbing the influence of youth religions and extremist sects.

Unfortunately the activities of external'Kidnapping/Deprogramming suppliers' cannot be completely avoided. However these acts are not supported by the German parent and concerned persons initiatives. It is also possible that there are individual persons who are inspiried by the American literature and who could be called 'wannabe' deprogrammers. Often, even the first impression which they make is so dubious that the shocked family members turn to one of the serious 'parent and concerned persons' initiatives.

Financing

NRM:

The financing of most of the youth religions and new religions is done everywhere mainly through so-called 'fundraising', more or less concealed ways of collecting money from outsiders.

To a lesser extent, the members and activists participate through fees and donations, however in some groups there is also voluntary work by the members of the organization.

The (exclusive) financing by dues, course fees, as well as licensing and franchising fees, seems to a very great extent, to function solely in Scientology, EST and Eckanker.

Financing of Parent and Concerned Persons Initiatives:

In Germany they are no longer supported by public (state) funds, but exclusively from donations and dues of the supporters. In some cases there is a small amount of support from the church.

Court trials[12]

Minor court cases involving fraud in collection methods or similar minor offences occur every now and then. In addition to that, problems involving new religions play a role in some civil cases, for example in cases of parental custody after a divorce. With the exception of suits against Scientology, demanding the repayment of course fees, there are few cases against the groups involving former members. Scientology usually tries to settle out of court, if a defeat is foreseeable, in order to avoid precedence cases.

Recently new religions and similar movements have tried to prevent critical comments by journalists, church commissioners, academics, and specialists in government positions by using the legal technique of 'temporal injunction.' Thus, a report from an inter-ministerial commission (consisting of representatives from different federal states) has not yet, after two years, been published because of a temporal injunctions instigated by various groups. The cooperation between the different groups in this area seems to be getting better and better.

However, because of the suits brought forward by various organizations, several courts in Germany have expressly confirmed the right of state authorities to inform about 'new religious and ideological movements and so-called psycho-groups'. They have even said this is a task for the Federal Government. Here are the various passages from the decision of the Supreme Court of the Federal Administrative Court:

As an organization of state leadership, it is part of the task of the Federal Government, as a principle, to continuously observe the development of society, to note misdevelopments or other problems quickly and exactly, to consider possibilities for prevention or rectification and to initiate necessary measures whether or not a resolution of the lawmaker is needed. (...) This task is namely given to the Federal Government in connection with certain social appearances, and this includes: the activities of groups described as 'youth religions' or 'youth sects' which are discussed with concern in public because the public especially under such conditions can expect to be informed on the information and viewpoint of the Federal Government. The fulfilment of this public need for information includes the possibility of state recommendations and warnings. (*BVerwG*, Decision from May 23rd, 1989).

One case which Transcendental Meditation brought against the Federal Government, because TM was mentioned in the first report of the Federal Government in 1978, lasted over ten years. This case ended with a defeat for the TM movement. The considerations regarding the state's right to make statements and warnings and the use of the term 'youth religions' are of considerable importance and thus will be presented here in detail.

On the one hand the respective groups claim that they are not religions, sects or ideologies at all and therefore should not be named or criticized in such a way or be considered in connection with other similar groups.

On the other hand such groups claim Article 4 of the Constitution and claim that as World View Communities or religions they even have special rights to be essentially exempt from criticism.

The TM movement even tried to combine both arguments.

Religious-ideological technique or not?[13]

In connection with claiming the state's neutrality obligation and a special protection of honour for the TM movement, the TM movement tried to claim for itself comprehensive protection under of Article 4 of the Constitution, the right to freedom of religious and ideological opinions (Art. 4, Section 1).

The Federal Administrative Court determined that on the one hand the 'communication and practice of a spiritual technique without specific spiritual content, or the granting of mere life-help' — which is the way TM presents itself, particularly in its advertising — is not protected under Art. 4, Section 1.

On the other hand, the plaintiffs according to their statements in the use of TM are also striving to achieve a continuous perfection of the world through the increase in the number of those who practice TM, and they are thus part of a worldwide movement in the service of a universal expectation of salvation, described by the term 'age of illumination': this ideological background of their doctrine speaks in favour of the granting of protection under Art. 4, Section 1 (Decision from May 23rd, 1989, (*BverwG* 7C 2.87, p. 23).

Without going into explanatory details about the contradiction — which is based on their own self-presentation — the Court nevertheless decided 'in favour of the plaintiff' stating that they are also under the protection of the Freedom of Opinion Article. However even this far-reaching protection cannot suffice to completely allow religious groups to be free from any form of criticism and warning, as the basic right expressed in Art. 4 of the Constitution is embedded in the totality of the constitutional regulations.

Freedom of opinion reaches its limitations especially there where the exercise of this basic right affects the human dignity and the right to life and freedom from bodily harm of other persons (decision from May 23rd, 1989, (*BverwG* 7C 2.87, p. 29).

Thus decided the Court in the TM decision.

Justification of Warnings of Danger:

The Federal Administrative Court in its decision of May 23rd, 1989 (*BverwG* 7C 2.87) also declared that the Federal Government's warnings against possible dangers from TM are justified. Because the meditation techniques taught by TM can lead to severe psychic disturbances among some unstable persons. The Federal Government is not only justified in issuing such warnings, but it is also their duty to observe social developments and prevent misdevelopments by way of such warnings.

If it is not to be denied that a psychically effective activitiy such as the TM technique could be a health hazard in any case for some unstable persons, it presents no extreme or unacceptable burden if from those who instruct others in this health-damaging technique, without having knowledge through a comprehensive training in the field of psychiatry or psychology in order to have defences against dangers, it is said he is not adequately qualifed as a teacher. (decision from May 23rd, 1989, *BverwG* 7C 2.87)

No Legal Right to Complain Regarding the Use of the Term 'Youth Religion':

One does not have the right to complain in court about the use of the term 'youth religion' or even 'psychosect' (cf. the following decision of May 23rd, 1989, *BverwG* 7C 2.87, p 32). On the one hand it is used by the Federal Government purely as a description, as a collective term for very different groups. It was pointed out in the publications of the Federal Government that along with some general characteristics, it is necessary to have a subtle and differentiated observation in order to avoid generalizations.This primarily descriptive use of the term does not contain significant interference of basic civil rights.

The differentiated presentation of the Federal Government was not satisfied with a general designation of the dangers, but went into the effects of the activities of each individual group.

The term 'youth religion', by the way, was not created by the Federal Government itself, but was found in the public discussion as a collective term for movements which are contemporaneous and are discussed in public with regard to their possible dangers. Inadmissable, and in some circumstances undesirable generalizations, from the Federal Government on the basis of their statement regarding the phenomenon could also, of course, have occurred with terms considered 'neutral.'

TM Reaction to the decision of the Federal Administrative Court:

The 'Society for Transcendental Meditation — German Association e.V.' reacted to this decision with a press release on June 2nd, 1989 in which it was stated that with the TM decision the Federal Administrative Court in Berlin had trampled on the law and order of the state and outraged and shocked thousands of citizens of the Federal Republic to the highest degree.'[14]

In the criticism of the decision they also state that:

Transcendental Meditation (TM) is an old and proven meditation technique which is practiced in the Federal Republic by approximately 100,000 people, and by approximately 3 million in about 110 nations of the world. In Germany, people who have learned TM include clergy of both confessions, hundreds of physicians, educators, lawyers, judges, civil servants, even a (former) presiding judge of the Federal Administrative Court, as well as a former Federal Chancellor [sic!].[15]

The German jurisdiction had 'completely lost its credibility among these citizens — and around the world'. Words such as 'perversion of the course of justice', 'prejudice', 'blindness towards justice', 'victory of ignorance and intolerance' were used in their criticism.

Constitutional Complaint of the TM Movement Rejected:

With a constitutional complaint, the TM movement tried to go to the Federal Constitutional Court to file suit against the decision of the Highest Administrative Court. In its complaint, the TM movement again tried to claim protection under Article 4 of the Constitution and referred to the state's neutrality obligation and tried to attack the use of the term 'youth religion' in connection with the TM movement in a report of the Federal Government and to attack the warnings of possible problems resulting from the TM movement.

However because of a lack of sufficient chance of success, this constitutional complaint was rejected with a decision of the First Chamber of the First Senate of the Constitutional Court (Bundesverfassungsgericht) on August 15th, 1989. In the reasons for rejection it was stated among other things (quoted in *NJW* 1989, Fascicle 51, 3268 ff) on the critical judgment of the appearance and influences of the TM movement by the Federal Government:

An accurate assessment in an actual regard to the objective appearance of the TM movement or its influences which must be ascribed to the complainant can also then not be an offence against honor when it, as here, leads to unfavourable results. (BVerfG. 1st Chamber of the First Senate) Decision from August 15th, 1989 — 1 BvR 881/89, quoted in *NJW* 1989, Fascicle 51, column 3270.

Is TM Religion?

Because the question is raised again and again whether TM is a religion, the following is an extensive quotation from the decision of the Federal Constitutional Court :

The C. (= complainants) themselves describe the doctrine they ascribe to as a 'closed system of thought which offers a basic concept for coping with human life in individual, social, and global realms'.

In the self-description of the TM movement, as in the texts published by Maharishi Mahesh Yogi, honoured as 'his holiness', and as can be noted in the material presented by the C., this system of thought is based on the old Indian veda. This is presented by the C. as a comprehensive structure of knowledge and understanding which is concerned with the basic principles of the cosmos and its gradual development into the visible creation.

The ideological foundation of the 'Science of Creative Intelligence' which reaches into the creation myths of Hinduism and is propagated by the TM movement, corresponds to a similarly comprehensive expectation of redemption or message of happiness which transcends the limits of human understanding and includes the entry into an 'Age of Illumination.'

In regard to the contents, foundations and eschatological perspectives of the 'Science of Creative Intelligence' and the trans- cendental meditation which is presented again and again in the public self-presentations and is developed more or less comprehensively, the C must accept that the principle which is for them binding, and supported with great effort in its totality, no longer is a pragmatic- technical instruction for coping with life, but is considered as a religion or religion-like world-view. Describing the TM movement as a 'youth sect' or 'youth religion' is not inappropriate for the ascribed objective representation of this movement to the extent in which personality rights are involved. (BVerfG. 1st Chamber for the First Senate, Decision of August 15th, 1989 — 1 BvR 881 /89, quoted in *NJW* 1989, Fascicle 51, column 3269.)

These groups who complained about state support to parent and concerned persons initiatives were successful in the end. The Federal Administrative Court decided that:

state authorities such as the Federal and Land Governments are allowed to make critical statements in regard to 'youth religions' and similar groups — an activity which, as with all state actions can be checked by the courts. However the state cannot delegate this task (also not in the form of financial support) without a legal basis, to parent initiatives or other free independent organizations, which are not subject to being checked by administrative jurisdiction. (*BVerfG.* from March 27th, 1992 7 C 21/90).

Police activities and the observations of the Acteurs

Police activity has occurred to a certain extent only in relation to the Krishna trial at the beginning of the 1970s. At that time, in addition to DM 800,000 of unclarified origin and destination, two pistols and two guns, as well as ammunition, were confiscated from the main Krishna temple in Germany. The then president of the temple took responsibility for the weapons cache and was sentenced to the minimum legal probationary term. At another trial at the Land Court in Frankfurt, the issue concerned other accusations and collection fraud. At a 'Scientific Conference' of the 'Academy for Vaishnava Culture' which belongs to ISKCON, and which was commemorating the 25th anniversary of ISKCON in

Germany, the organization for the first time, took a self-critical position regarding the ownership of weapons and collection fraud.

Sukrita Dasa, the Director of the legal department of ISKCOM Germany, in a self-critical article begins by saying:[16]

The fact that also in the time afterwards there was not a self-critical reflection in the Hare-Krishna movement is seen (today) by the divinely enlightened as a shortcoming, with which this work can be helped a bit.

In their decision of April 28th, 1978, the *Land* Court in Frankfurt determined considerable causes for complaint regarding the collection methods of ISKCON. It was stated:

As all money movement took place through the associations of the ISKCON, an independent economic activity of the aid society could not be determined.

Today the ISKCON maintain that their problems from that time have been solved and they are on the road to recovery: *In hindsight we must say that we repeatedly make great errors in dealing with the public, with families and with institutions.*[17]

Also, some of the other 'errors' which used to be vehemently denied are today indirectly called by name and thus their former practice is admitted. In this way they confirm the addition of other points to what was formerly considered 'intolerant' criticism:

Minors are only allowed to join a temple community with the expressed written permission of their parents. Today we no longer encourage anyone to discontinue their education.

We will have to wait and see how the development continues. In any case it seems that the German ISKCON, after the second conference, has detached itself from the cartel of 'youth religions' and other ideological extremist groups. It seems to be that the ISKCON no longer participates in these conferences, at which especially the Moon movement and Scientology discuss their strategies.

Notes

1. Friedrich-Wilhelm Haack, *Die neuen Jugendreligionen* Munich 1988: Part 1. 24th edition. (The definitive publication through which the phenomenon and the term 'youth religion' became publicly known. The book continues to be revised and presents the most current information.) Friedrich-Wilhelm Haack, *Die neuen Jugendreligionen* Munich, 1991: Part 5. Gurubewegungen und Psychoculte — Durchblicke und Informationen.

2. For the popular and not unimportant 'mapping', here are two recommendations which are not only for the German language area: Oswald Eggenberger, *Die Kirchen, Sondergruppen und religiösen Vereinigungen*, Zurich 1990, 5th revised edition. Friedrich-Wilhelm Haack, Findungshilfe Religion 2000: *Apologetisches Lexikon. Aktivitäten, Ereignisse, Firmen, Gruppen Institutionen, Orden und Personen im Zusammenhang mit religiösen und weltanschaulichen Bewegungen — ein fragmentarischer Überblick*. Munich, 1990: Material-Edition 28 der ARW.

3. Cf.: Friedrich-Wilhelm Haack, *Scientology — Magie des 20. Jahrhunderts*. Munich 1991, 2nd ed. (standard work). Friedrich-Wilhelm Haack and Thomas Gandow, *Scientology, Dianetik und andere Hubbardismen*, Munich 1993, 3rd expanded edition.

4. Cf.: Thomas Gandow, *Mun-Bewegung: CARP, CAUSA und die 'Vereinigungskirche' des San Myung Mun*, Munich, 1993. Friedrich-Wilhelm Haack, *Das Mun-Imperium/Beobachtungen — Informationen Meinungen* (Findungshilfe Mun-Bewegung) Munich, 1991, Materialedition 31 der ARW.

5. For a long time the most prominent member of the Moon movement in Germany was Ursula Saniewski, who then belonged to the leadership of the right wing 'Republikaner' Party and according to information of the Social Democratic Press Service 'Blick nach rechts' from February 1994 represents the party chairman Schönhuber as publisher and editor-in-chief of the party publication 'Der Republikaner'.

6. Friedrich-Wilhelm Haack and Thomas Gandow, *Transzendentale Meditation*, Munich: 1992, 6th expanded ed.

7. Another area which will not be covered here but which is not unimportant is the increasing occultism among young people and young adults. There is an excellent study done by the Berlin specialist for religious studies: Hartmut Zinser, *Jugendokkultismus in Ost und West. Vier quantitative Untersuchungen 1989-1991*. Ergebnisse — Tabellen — Analysen, Munich, 1993, ARW.

8. Kurt Hutten, (Hg Reimer, D.), *Seher, Grübler, Enthusiasten*. Das Buch der traditionellen Sekten u. religiösen Sonderbewegungen: Stuttgart, 1982, 12th ed.

9. Horst Reller, and Manfred Kiessig, (eds.): *Handbuch Religiöse Gemeinschaften, Freikirchen, Sondergemeinschaften, Sekten, Weltanschauungen, missionierende Religionen des Ostens, Neureligionen*. Gütersloh: 1993, 4th completely revised and expanded edition.

10. Hans Gasper, et al (eds.): *Lexikon der Sekten, Sondergruppen und Weltanschauungen*, Freiburg: 1990, Herder-Verlag.

11. Cf. G. Lanczkowski, *Die neuen Religionen*, Hamburg 1974. C. Colpe, Synkretismus, Renaissance, Säkularisation und Neubildung von Religionen in der Gegenwart, in: *Handbuch der Religionsgeschichte*, edited by J.P. Asmussen and J. Laessoe in cooperation with C. Colpe, Göttingen: 1971-1975, Vol. 3, p. 444 pp. In the field of the sociology of religion, see especially the works by M. Schibilsky, *Religiöse Erfahrung und Interaktion, Die Lebenswelt jugendlicher Randgruppen*, Stuttgart 1976, and others.

12. A good basic overview regarding legal issues involved in new religious groups can be found in: Herberg Taudien, *Grenzen der Religionsfreiheit*. Rechtliche Möglichkeiten zur Reaktion auf die Aktivitäten neuerer religiöser Begwegungen. Münchener Texte und Analysen zur Religiösen Situation, epv. Munich 1987.

13. The account here follows for the most part the publication of F.W. Haack and Thomas Gandow: *Transzendentale Meditation*, Maharishi Mahesh Yogi-Maharishi Veda, Münchener Reihe 1992.

14. The German jurisdiction has failed miserably! Press information of the 'Society for Transcendental Meditation — German Assoc. e.V.' from June 2, 1989, p. 2)

15. The account here follows for the most part the publication of F.W. Haack and Thomas Gandow: *Transzendentale Meditation*, Maharishi Mahesh Yogi-Maharishi Veda, Münchener Reihe 1992.

16. Sukrita dasa: Der Rettershof-Prozess aus heutiger Sicht, in: Akademie für Vaishnava-Kultur (ed.) *25 Jahre ISKCON — Deutschland*. Konferenz der Akademie für Vaishnava-Kultur on January 29, 1994 in Wiesbaden, pp. 49.

17. Daya Devi Dasi, Tempelpräsidentin der ISKCON-Wiesbaden, 'ISKCON Deutschland: Rückblick und Ausblick' in: Akademie für Vaishnava-Kultur (ed.) *25 Jahre ISKCON — Deutschland*, Konferenz der Akademie für Vaishnava-Kultur on January, 29, 1994 in Wiesbaden, p. 57.

CHAPTER 11

New Religious Movements in Austria

by Friederike Valentin

It has been said that the Austrians are not the type to create a new heresy or to believe in it. In fact, only a few sects or new religious movements originate in Austria. In the last century Jakob Lorber lived in a part of the former Austrian Empire, and Rudolf Steiner, the founder of Anthroposophy, grew up in Austria and lived in Vienna for 10 years. Some 100 years ago the 'Austrian Shakespeare', Franz Grillparzer, said: 'The Austrians hold their peace and let the others talk'. Nevertheless, in Austria there are many different religious groups and movements outside the Churches.

To understand the religious landscape I want to point out that Austria is mainly a Catholic country (78% in 1991). People who don't belong to one of the officially recognized religious denominations total more than 100,000 and sometimes are seen as the second biggest 'denominational' group. Sects and New Religious Movements are a minority and are often regarded as outsiders by society.

Vienna has a special position as a melting pot between East and West. Vienna is also a melting pot in a cultural way by the presence of the different nations of the old Austrian-Hungarian Empire. In those days Vienna was seen (and saw itself) as an edge of the Balkans — and in recent decades as the end of the Western world. But after the fall of the Iron Curtain in 1989 a new way of communication started — not only between nations but also between different religious groups. For example, the Scientology Organization in Vienna gave aid to 'the Org' in Budapest. On the other hand some sects (e.g. Mormons and Jehovah's Witnesses) offer their service and literature to people from Hungary and Czechoslovakia in their mother tongue.

The religious landscape — an overview

Groups in conflict with the Catholic Church

In Austria the foundation of the Opus Angelorum took place. It was founded by a Tyrolean housewife, Gabriele Bitterlich, shortly after the Second World War. The headquarters of this international movement is near Innsbruck (St. Petersberg, Silz). In this organization there are a number of secret books which are derived from the gnostic-cabbalistic orientation. The organization has been cautioned twice by the Vatican regarding practices and teachings. The Tyrolean bishop as well as the Austrian Bishops' Conference also condemned these questionable acivities. The group gathering around Mgr. Lefebvre has also some centres in Austria. In 1989 they took over a church in the city of Salzburg. The organization of Clemente Dominguez who declares himself as the true pope (Gregor XII) has some small centres in Austria.

Evangelicals and Pentecostals

There are more than 50 different evangelical (fundamentalist) organizations which are partly working together with the Lutheran Church and are also in connection with the Evangelical Alliance. Generally they are against ecumenism and have built up their own platform, the 'Reichgottes-Arbeiter-Tagung'. There are also several American missionaries active. Since 1972 nearly 110 evangelical communities have been founded. Their members are mostly Anabaptist.

There are two big neo-Pentecostal missionary movements active in Austria: 'Youth with a Mission' and 'Full Gospel Business Men International'. The former group tries to get in touch with the official Churches, the other is building up its own communities and is also re-baptizing. In general there is a significant increase in Pentecostal communities which see themselves as 'non-denominational', (e.g. Vineyard).

'Classical' Sects

The Mormons and the New Apostolic Church are officially recognized. Seventh-Day-Adventists still do not always declare themselves. Sometimes their means of propaganda are seminars for better health ('Liga Leben und Gesundheit').

Jehovah's Witnesses (approx. 20,000 members) are well known to the public because of their aggressive and intensive mission. Some years ago an Austrian Court jugded that in case of divorce the children involved should grow up with the parent who is not a member of the Jehovah's Witnesses, for two reasons: 1) endangering health by refusing blood transfusions and 2) social isolation. In 1993 Strasbourg reversed this resolution. Some weeks later a 10-day old baby died because its parents refused the necessary blood transfusion. This led to an intensive media reaction concerning not only the Jehovah's Witnesses but also sects in general. Jehovah's Witnesses are trying to become officially recognized.

A small group of the Norwegian Brothers (Smithians) received publicity after a deprogramming. A mother tried to let her adult daughter be deprogrammed by Ted Patrick. The court sentenced the mother for depriving her daughter of the constitutional rights of the individual. Thereupon the mother went to the Court of Appeal. The case is still in progress.

Esoterism

Anthroposophy is spreading by its practice, especially its educational model (Waldorfschulen), its health service and the health food produced by the 'Biologisch-Dynamischer Landbau'. New revelations are following the ideas of Lorber (e.g., H. Kohler). The 'Liga fur Parapsychologische Forschung' was founded in Vienna in 1948; Gisela Weidner is editing these 'revelations'. Universelles Leben (the former 'Heimholungswerk Jesu Christ') has periodical meetings in 15 towns and villages. Fiat Lux has a centre in Carinthia (Sittersdorf) and another near Vienna and is offering lectures in towns. New Age is widespread since the 1980's. There are some 100 different centrers all over the country. There is an increasing interest in archaic religiosity (e.g. Shamanism, Celts, Druids).

Occultism

Spiritism is growing in different ways, not only among students. Channeling is used by a branch of the New Age Movement. In

1993 the small centre 'LichtOase' in Rannariedl, upper Austria, was involved in a court case and as a result moved to Great Britain. In this 'LichtOase' Julie Ravel claims to channel 'Ramtha'. Satanism is also practised in various small circles. In 1989 three young men from one village committed suicide. To all appearances they'd had some contact with such a circle. The increase in youth Satanism is an alarming signal.

New Religious Movements

The Unification Church has existed since 1966. In 1974 the 'Holy Spirit Association for the Unification of World Christianity', recognized as an association, was officially dissolved. Thereupon they went underground and were successful in recruiting members. Now their status is 'Gesellschaft burgerlichen Rechts' but with no official recognition. As in other countries they are established economically in different activities (e.g., 'Saeilo', candle manufacturing 'P. Koch', producing and selling software 'Fa. Resperger', export and import 'Multifa' carpentry 'Tischlerei Ottel', selling homemade woodcarvings 'Schnitzerei Blassnig'). There are also a number of organizations, e.g. Forum ost, Forum Religion und Weltgestaltung, Forum Osterreich, CAUSA, Frauenföderation, or Familienföderation, für Weltfrieden and RYS.

The Austrian training centre ('Schmied an der Strass', Gaflenz) is led by a former Catholic priest and Benedictine friar (Heinz Krcek). The Moonies took public advantage of this fact by sending letters to parishes. In general Moonies make special efforts trying to contact priests. In 1993 another Catholic priest joined the Moonies.

The Children of God/The Family are active in the underground. In Advent 1989 they gave a small concert in an institution for aged people, sold their music cassettes and distributed posters with the impress 'CAMU'.

A number of guru-movements are active. Since 1975 Transcendental Meditation is established in Austria. To all appearances they are influential on the political level by their 'Arztegemeinschaft fur TM'. The small group of followers of Sri Chinmoy organizes many seminars on meditation and occasionally a 'Weltfriedenslauf' and other initiatives for world peace. The Sewa-shops belong to them. Brahma Kumaris is offering workshops. In 1989 the 'Global Co-Operation for a Better World' organized a seminar on economics and spirituality at Vienna University. The different groups of Sant Mat (Thakar Singh, Rajinder Singh, Unity of Man) have been active for several years. Nirmala Devi and her Sahaja Yoga is well established and runs about 20 centres all over Austria. Ananda Marga has only a few members in Austria. They were present at the 'Esoterik-Messe' in Vienna.

Neue Akropolis has been active for more than 10 years and has some centres throughout Austria. They offer different lectures on esoteric subjects. Sometimes they react very aggressively to critical information.

Scientology is well established, being active for more than 20 years. The biggest centre is in Vienna. There are other centres, e.g. in Carinthia. There are also several peppermint-organizations, e.g. 'Pädagogische Institute', Narconon, which is also active. In Vienna Scientologists have started to run a small school named the 'Creative College' (not recognized by the educational authorities). Scientologists are also active in the field of marketing and management (e.g. U-Man and Business Success). In 1991 the Austrian Government denied Scientology the status of a non-profit organization. Scientology gave notice of appeal against that judgment. In 1995 the Court in Vienna *(Unabhängiger Verwaltungs-senat)* decided that Scientology is to be seen as a religion and therefore as a non-profit organization. There are several splinter groups of Scientology, e.g. Advanced Ability Centre and ex-Scientologists who depend on Ron's Org, or Dianasis.

Native Austrian New Religious Movements

The most important locally born new religious movement is the AAO (Aktionsanalytische Organization) founded by Otto Muhl. The international centre of that organization was the Friedrichshof in Burgenland near the Hungarian border. The Friedrichshof is juridically a cooperative society ('Gemeinnutzige Wohn-Bau- und Siedlungsgenossenschaft') and has had its own primary school with public recognition. Otto Muhl and his wife Claudia were convicted of crimes in 1992; since then the AAO has lost its importance.

In 1978 Gottfried Holic (who studied Theology for more than 20 years) started his mission which is focused on rejection of the churches. The members see themselves as the only true Christians

('Wahre Christen'). They tried to recruit members by going day by day to Christian groups and speaking to people trying to make them 'true' Christians. Because of their extreme lifestyle (e.g. lack of sleep and malnutrition in their communities) this group is judged as a new religious movement.

In 1981 a mother tried to get her daughter out by deprogramming but failed. Since 1989 this organization has been active in Hungary and other former Eastern States and the groups there have expanded rapidly.

General remarks

About 100,000 members are estimated to be in nearly 700 various groups and movements and some 100,000 are additionally interested in these ideas. According to the European Values Survey Study (see p. 14), about 20% of Austrians believe in reincarnation.

In general we have two tendencies: On one hand there is a trend to Christian fundamentalism and to strongly organized groups; on the other hand a trend towards New Age esoterism and groups without any firm connections.

Reactions

In 1953 the Roman Catholic Church established the present 'Referat fur Weltanschauungsfragen, Sekten und religiöse Gemeinschaften' for the purpose of giving information and support. In 1976 the work started on a cross-diocesean level. Now, in every diocese there is a deputy. The Referat fur Weltanschauungsfragen publishes leaflets and booklets (*Werkmappe Sekten, religiöse Sondergemeinschaften, Weltanschauungen*) and collaborates in publishing an encyclopedia on this subject (*Lexikon der Sekten, Sondergruppen und Weltanschauungen,* Hans Gasper, Joachim Muller, Friederike Valentin; 4th edition, Freiburg: Herder, 1992).

The Lutheran Church started a similar work in 1975. There is a very good cooperation on the ecumenical level. As early as 1980 a declaration on sects and cults was published on an ecumenical level ('Kirchliche Stellungnahme zur Frage der Sekten') and was widely distributed.

A special institute researching parapsychology and occult phenomena was established in Innsbruck and is led by P. Dr

Andreas Resch. He publishes a periodical, *Grenzgebiete der Wissenschaft*.

Since 1982 the state has shown a large interest in the subject, which has led to some sort of cooperation between the state, the Catholic and Lutheran Churches and the Austrian Parents' Association. Thus, for example, a booklet was published by the Ministry of Education in spring 1982. It was titled 'Die pseudoreligiösen Aussteiger — Jugendreligionen in Österreich' (The pseudo-religious dropouts — Cults in Austria). A second edition was published by the Ministry of Education and the Ministry of Youth and Family in 1987 and was titled 'Jugendreligionen — Psychokulte — Gurubewegungen'. As a result of this study, Scientology went to court but without success. In this second edition there is no information concerning AAO and TM. It is evident that these groups are supported in part by politically influential persons. In 1993 a hearing was held in Parliament which subsequently led to several official questions in the House.[1]

The Austrian Parents' Association ('Gesellschaft gegen Sekten und Kultgefahren') was founded in Vienna in 1977 and is called 'Verein zur Wahrung der geistigen Freiheit — gesamtösterreichische Elterninitiative' (Foundation for Keeping Mental Freedom — All-Austrian Parents' Organization). There are about 130 members. The organization is financially supported by the local authorities.

Notes

1. In 1996 a new booklet was published by the Ministry for Family (Sekten-Wissen Schübl). This paper has attained a large circulation (approx. 250,000) within five months.

CHAPTER 12

Denmark and Scandinavia vis-à-vis New Religious Movements

Johannes Aagaard

Scandinavia, particularly Denmark, has social structures, both economic and cultural, which tend to reward conformity and to downplay dissidence and nonconformity. Much of that conformist tendency holds true for Danish religious practices: for example, movements which are antagonistic towards the culture and propose alternative societies — such as Bhagwan Osho, Hare Krishna, Ananda Marga — or even those which support ideas of a dominating society through a universal religious government such as Transcendental Meditation, have not enjoyed much support in Denmark. Those same movements do, however, have successful centres and programmes just across the southern Danish border in Germany. In Denmark the decisive factor that determines a group's likelihood of success, barring mismanagement and inept leadership, is the movement's religious conformity to general social rather than Judeo-Christian norms. Christianity, the sentimental favourite, has less than two percent of the population actively engaged in Sunday worship, that is, church attendance more than five times a year. Nevertheless, in the 1990s student enrolment in theological studies is surging upward, and a general increase of interest and activism in Christianity can be seen.[1]

A revived notion of religious life may be at hand in Denmark which could possibly also benefit new religions that have been active here for some 25 years. Some surveys suggest that between 20% and 30% of the Danish population accepts belief in reincarnation, a distinctly Hindu-Buddhist-Theosophical view popularized in recent decades. Eastern guru movements — such as Swami Narayanananda with his Yoga-trust, Swami Janakananda with his Scandinavian Yoga — have had the most impact on Danes in the 70s and 80s, though groups of an esoteric and/or gnostic origin, and healing/terapeutic movements — such as Alice Bailey and Ananda Tara Shan — have become vogue.

Movements which have attracted significant media attention in Europe have operations in Denmark, both in the Copenhagen area, which is residence for 1.3 million Danes, and the city of Aarhus, a community of 250,000. Copenhagen is the point of entry for most new religions which, if successful, establish centres in other areas of the country. Scientology, Transcendental Meditation (TM), the Tongil Family (known elsewhere as the Unification Church), ISKCON, and the Children of God (Family of Love, Magic of Heaven/World Service, The Family) all have a presence in Copenhagen.

In fact, one can now find over 300 addresses in the Copenhagen telephone directory for offices, centres, and business enterprises that are related to the new religious movements.

Scientology and TM have been especially active throughout Denmark, with some measure of success achieved by both. Scientology has translated the fundamental works of L. Ron Hubbard into Danish, and TM's material, as well as that of Scientology are popularly promoted through retail bookstores.

Both movements are concerned about their present image in Denmark, however. Scientology, an active loser in litigation against critics, has failed to effectively communicate their unusual campaigns to help society, most notably the attempt to condemn as 'deleterious' the prescribing by psychiatrists of drugs or electrotherapy for their patients. Furthermore, the loss of Hubbard's leadership, which has caused large fissures in Scientology, with breakaway groups forming new organizations but retaining identical belief systems, brings pressure on Danish Scientology to hold on to its core groups of members. Scientology manages to recruit some new members, but the statistics of the back door are often as high as the statistics of the front door. In Norway the ex-members have been able to get large sums of money back from Scientology by means of court cases. In that light, Scientology members have been actively campaigning for recruits by button-holing people on the street, offering to administer personality tests at their nearby offices. Recently Scientology has established itself as management specialists and promoters of business expansion in many branches of business.

TM, on the other hand, has not suffered internal disorganization in Denmark. But in Norway ACEM stands for the free

TM meditation movement. The Sidhi programme (levitation) however has damaged the image of TM as such. TM is growing more in Sweden than elsewhere in Scandinavia. Its emphasis is now generally on the Ayurvedic medicine and the general miraculous influence from the TM meditation, which they see as the reason behind the changing world situation, first of all the breakdown of Communism. The same pretension is expressed by other cults, such as the Unification Church, whose master Moon is promoting himself as the spiritual leader of the new European House. This 'church' has reduced its activities in Scandinavia in order to strengthen the expansion in Russia and Eastern Europe.

Hare Krishna (ISKCON), though an Eastern movement which is successful in other European settings, has not been able to establish security or influence in Denmark. In spite of their resources and organizational skill, ISKCON looks like many other small religious groups in Denmark — a collection of eager hopefuls with an exaggerated view of their importance. Found mainly in Copenhagen, Krishnas illustrated their ambiguous position when they applied for recognition from the Ministry for Church Affairs, an agency that grants permission to perform marriages. The application was rejected when it was discovered that ISKCON's number of adherents, reported to be several hundred, were dinner-club members, and that in reality there were only a dozen committed Krishna devotees. Now there are about 50, but not very well committed members. ISKCON's lack of success in Denmark is also distinctly related to their rejection of the Danish culture, as they accept only the culture of India.

Another Eastern movement — the radical, militant Ananda Marga, once led by Ananda Murti — suffers a similar lack of appreciation in Denmark because its radical agenda and rejection of society requires Danes to disown their society and heritage, an act Danes are reluctant to perform. Its political headquarters (PROUT) was for many years situated in Copenhagen, from where this worldwide movement was administered.

The Children of God, though Western and vaguely related to Christianity, present the same liability to Danish recruits, but small numbers have joined, leaving distresssed families behind. Some of them departed for other countries such as India and Argentina and the Far East (Hong Kong, Macao) but they have now come back. 'The Family', so-called, is working under the cover of post office boxes, hiding their address and identity. But they seem to have stabilized their presence in Scandinavia once more, but very much reduced in numbers.

The Tongil Family/Unification Church/the Moonies, in many ways are exactly opposite the Children of God, but in fact they often represent the same tendency of alternative and sectarian escape from society. In spite of small numbers and repeated organizational breakdowns, the 'Moonies' have attracted more attention than any other group in Denmark. This is true in spite of the fact that they have very few actual members. The campaign of the Dialogue Centre against them has had a strong effect and has somehow isolated them.

Together with Scientology, the Moonies have created front organizations with different names which have harassed, and tried to pacify, all critical minds who have dared to make unfavourable remarks about the many new religious movements.

Successful groups do abound in Denmark, nonetheless. They include the meditation schools inspired by Narayanananda (he died in 1989), an Indian guru with impressive ashram properties in 25 locations throughout Denmark, and Swami Janakananda of the Scandinavian Yoga School, himself a Scandinavian, who runs an equal number of Danish centres inspired originally by swami Satyananda from the Bihar School of Yoga. Both movements, like a number of small meditation movements, develop loose bonds of affiliation which allow Danes both to freely pursue cultural interests and join an ashram for a monastic commitment when they want. Some Hindu meditation movements have sponsored art shows and craft displays to prove their interest in the culture.

By far, the Hatha Yoga meditation schools are the largest and most effective vehicle by which Neo-Hinduism is communicated in Denmark. The various Hatha Yoga Schools, frequently led by teachers who are actively committed to a Hindu world view, sponsor classes (predominantly within the system of adult education in Denmark), which, if attended by a quorum of students, receive a generous government subsidy. This is so because the yoga schools maintain that they have 'nothing to do with religion', a statement which is obviously false. Some of the Danish folk high schools function as yoga sponsors. Basic Hatha Yoga classes teach the breathing methods so important to distinctly religious yogic techniques; and they function as natural bridges to Tantric Yoga. Adept students, pursuing their successful experiences in Hatha

Yoga, can easily find excellent recources for more intense, advanced techniques and possible philosophic interpretations.

Danish Tantra schools, which are devoted to the Tantric practices of an accepted and respected Hindu religiosity in India, persistently claim that they are not Hindus and not religious. Rather, they say their practices are primal expressions of trans-religious knowledge, beyond religion. Beside the popularity of Janakananda and Narayananada are a host of smaller yoga movements inspired by others, for example Bhagwan Rajneesh — known in his last months as 'Osho'. An offshoot of his movement is led by Michael Barnett under the name 'The Wild Goose' or the Heart of the Sun. Also worth mentioning are Sri Ram Chandra, Sathya Sai Baba, Yogi Bhajan of the Happy, Healthy, Holy Organization (3HO), and Eckankar. Other movements exist on a small scale: Sri Chinmoy, Chidvilasananda (Muktananda's aristocratic successor) and the Brahma Kumaris.

Eastern movements in Denmark present an option for meditators to go beyond limitations which the mundane world applies to daily life. TM's Sidhi programme, which offers 'powers of invincibility, invisibility, levitation, the strength of elephants, and a tranquil calm', is a clear example. On the other hand, the Divine Light Mission — known now as Elan Vitale — founded by Guru Maharaj Ji, is a demythologized movement that has lost its ability to recruit members. Maharaj Ji, by his own wish is no longer a guru, neither is he a master. His new role as a guide is vague and not very well understood by members and outsiders who have seen him reduced from Lord of the Universe to a modest spiritual counsellor.

Japanese new religions are coming more and more to the forefront, but are still small, such as Mahikari, Soka Gakkai (lay organization of Nichiren Shoshu) Rissho Kosei Kai, and Reiki, the last being quite succesful in the 90s.

General occult and spiritist tendencies have grown stronger all over Scandinavia and they have attracted much attention of media reports and public awareness which has also created a market for publications about those and similar movements. Menos, an occult group which promotes a hightech version of self-deification, and Factum Humanum (the White Order) are heavily spiced with esotericism and secret rituals. In spite of critical public evaluation, both have survived, but not without difficulty.

Anthroposophy, founded by Rudolf Steiner in the early 1900s, has so successfully integrated itself into Danish society that, in spite of broad esotericism and unusual, unfounded interpretations of the Bible, associating it with new religions is greeted with surprise and some appreciation. Anthroposophy's Waldorf schools are exceedingly popular, and building programmes have continued but with some recession. Members make occasional excursions to take upper-echelon courses offered at the Goetheanum, the international headquarters and the site of Anthroposophy's School of Spiritual Science, located near Basel, Switzerland. Anthroposophy also sponsors an extended social programme similar to Britain's Camphill Communities for disabled children, although that name is not used in Denmark.

Subtler forms of occultism are introduced via the Rosicrucians (first of all AMORC), the adherents of Martinus, the Towards the Light Movement, and the Gurdjieff-inspired Linbu centres. Those groups lead rather quiet lives, yet they are steadfast within their own esoteric walls.

The traditional theosophists (Adyar type) are not numerous in Denmark any more, but other theosophical offshoots prosper, such as The Alice Bailey Organizations (The Lucis Trust, World Goodwill, Triangles, The Great Invocation); also Elisabeth Claire Prophet-activities florish (The Summit Lighthouse, Church Universal and Triumphant, Keepers of the Flame). Ananda Tara Shan units (Rosenhaven, Shan International, Society for Maitreya Theosophy) which are now expanding in Australia and the USA.

Christian-related movements such as American imports like the Worldwide Church of God and The Way International, are hidebound by their supporting cultural baggage, which limits their potential appeal to Danes. Nevertheless, their outposts are maintained here, as they are in other parts of Europe, but in the last years in turmoil and under reform.

Other movements like the Mormons and Jehovah's Witnesses prosper all over Denmark, but their basic occult nature has become more and more obvious. In spite of that — or because of that — they continue to grow. New success-religions like *Livets Ord* (Word of Life) have also caught fire in Denmark. In Sweden and Norway however, they have established themselves solidly. The Local Church (Witness Lee) has not managed to break out of the limitations of two small congregations but could do so any time. The Local Church has been hit by a serious split. Its European organization has separated from the International organization, and the reason is first of all a critique of Witness Lee and his despotical behaviour. Their devastating and cruel campaign against the late Neil Duddy is now to some extent recognised to be unjust and abnominable.

Other groups like the Satanists which have existed in Denmark for some time, present a startling image — in heavy-metal rock for instance. Erwin Neutzsky-Wulff — a well-known author in Denmark — presents a sophisticated version of general occultism with some Satanic characteristics.

A very special expression of perverted religiousity is found in the many 'popular' satanic phenomena. Scandinavia has been hit by a large number of Satanist actions of violence, first of all harming and violating churches and cemeteries. Both ecclesiastical and secular authorities have tended to hide such actions from the public. The idea is that publicity might promote such violence. This is, however, a matter for discussion as is the idea that young, confused people are the only agents of satanism. In fact a number of networks seem to promote the Satanist activities, and in some cases it has been obvious that also stable and established Satanic lodges have been active. The general influence of heavy-metal music is also to be studied as a source of satanic attitudes as is satanic literature. Not least LaVey's publications seem to be responsible for a number of satanic expressions of aggression.

In the past years healing and therapy have come to the fore-front. Many campaigns such as 'Healing Explosion' are manifested with a 'Christian' life-style which is startling and provocative. Others are far beyond any Christian definition, although they pretend to be true Christianity, such as the various sorts of channelling, A Course in Mircacles, and Foundation for Inner Peace.

In the occult versions of healing the Energy is disguised as Kundalini-power, which is able to take its adherents not only to perfect health but also to divinity beyond the mortal sphere. Under the headings of 'healing' or 'Spiritual growth', a widespread network of local centres have come into being. The discussion about alternative medicine has become a national event in nearly all newspapers and mass-communication systems.

In the period during which astrology has risen up and in which the astrologers have become more or less accepted parts of business and management, most of the new religious movements have accepted an overall myth in the form of the NEW AGE. The basis is astrological and the context is occult, while the thinking is gnostic mediated by various theosophical movements. In this form the new religiosity has been able to establish an influence far beyond the relatively limited new religious groups.

Latin American groups are also found in Scandinavia. The new Acropolis is advertizing its gnostic message, the Arica is going forward again and SILO is communicating his communitarian message which is transformed into politics in the Humanistic Party, which is popping up unsuccessful now and again.

New Age is in the air to such an extent that no one can maintain that they are not influenced by it. It is in the music, it is in the art, it is in the radio and TV and newspapers and the weekly magazines, as a wave of new spirituality and new super-stition. In management and industry and among the middle- aged academic elite, various undefined mystery religions prosper, sometimes combined with drugs such as ecstasy, the successor of LSD in the sixties.

There are signs that the oriental spirituality is fusing with traditional Danish folk-religiosity, turning against Christianity, which is described as a life-negating religion. The New Age ideology understands itself as holistic, while Christianity is caricatured as dualistic. In fact holism in this context means monism, since the emphasis is on the identity of everything: There is no difference! Consequently the growth and expansion of consciousness is seen as an essential task, while 'conscience' is interpreted as a Christian aberration.

The two main figures in the intellectual part of New Age in Denmark are the Irishman Bob Moore, whose basis is Theosophy, and Jes Bertelsen, originally a disciple of Bob Moore, but now becoming more and more Tantric, but also expressing a search for Eastern Orthodox spirituality. Their disciples are found in numerous growth centres all over Denmark. The study of New Age has just begun, but it seems that the following generalisation may be made: New Age is the soft occultisation of Christianity.

In mentioning the indigenous beliefs, certain worship practices in Denmark's former protectorate, Iceland, come to mind. In the 60s and 70s there was a revival of an ancient Nordic religion, Asatru, wherein people gathered to offer animal sacrifices to Nordic gods such as Freya and Thor. However, this is probably more of a 'happening' than a religious reality, and although relatively few people are in fact involved in this ancient Nordic religion, Asatru is now spreading to all Scandinavian Countries, especially Norway in the form of neo-paganism.

One possible concluding remark could be this: Eastern religions in Denmark are the dominant new religions of the 90s. Movements of lesser substance, with no real traditional background, come and go, but the guru movement, it seems, will abide. The Hindu Visva Parishad, an umbrella organization, tries to bring the various Hindu groups together. These Hindu (and Buddhist) movements are not strictly speaking new religious movements, for their substance is more or less the same as traditional Hinduism and Buddhism. This is obviously the case with the Tibetan, the Vietnamese, and the Thai Buddhists, who are to be found in Denmark following their own different versions. The Tibetan Buddhists mainly identify themselves within the Kagyud-pa tradition, Karmapa-branch, while a smaller group goes for the Gelug-pa, Dalai Lama branch. Such Buddhists do not recruit any longer from the alternative scene only. Even on the top level of society their influence is felt. The Vietnamese Buddhists are slowly finding their way into a Danish lifestyle. They recently called a monk to begin the Buddhist Sangha. They are, however, scattered all over the country and often in isolation from the population as such. The same is true for the Tamil-refugees, especially from Sri Lanka, who are mainly Hindus, and the Thai immigrants, who have established two Thai-Buddhist centres in Copenhagen.

Notes

1. A special initiative in Denmark *The Dialog Centre* has grown into an international enterprise called *Dialog Centre International* with units in about 20 countries in Europe and South-East Asia. This network of DCI mainly operates by means of modern technology. (Its Internet address is http://www.dci.dk). It also publishes magazines such as Den Nye Dialog (in Danish), Spirituality in East and West (in English), and Berliner Dialog (in German). The address of DCI is, Katrinebjergvej 46, 8200, Aarhus N, Denmark — Telephone 0045 86 10 54 11, fax: 0045 86 10 54 16. e-mail: info @ dci.dk.

About the Authors

Johannes Monrad Aagaard
Professor for Missiology and Ecumenical Theology, The Theological Faculty, University of Aarhus, Denmark. President for The Dialogue Centre International. Editor of *Spirituality in East and West, The New Dialogue, Buddhist Christian Dialogue Information.* Author of various books on missiology and dealing with theological studies of religion and with ecumenical studies.

Antonios Alevisopoulos (died May 1996)
Dr Theol., Dr Phil. Father Antonios Alevisopoulos was advisor of the Holy Synod of the Church of Greece regarding matters of cults and sects. Director of the Office of Archdiocese of Athens for matters of Information, Dialogue and Culture. President of the Inter-Orthodox Parents' Initiatives Association. Studied Theology at the University of Athens. Philosophy, Ecclesiastical History and Slavic Literature at the University of Mainz. Since 1968 was involved in educational and training programmes on behalf of the Orthodox Church of Greece (Orthodox Theological Seminar etc.) and coordinated the Pan-Orthodox cooperation for pastoral confrontation of the contemporary sects.

Gianni Ambrosio
Co-authored the paper on Italy, is a Roman Catholic priest active in the pastoral ministry in the diocesis of Vercelli and a professor of Sociology of Religion at the Northern University of Theology in Milan. He is the author of a number of essays on religious liberty, new religious movements and the sociology of religions in general.

Eileen Barker
Eileen Barker is Professor of Sociology with Special Reference to the Study of Religion at the London School of Economics, and is currently Head of the Department of Sociology. For the last 25 years she has been researching new religious movements and has over 120 scholarly publications to her name. These include: *The making of a Moonie: Brainwashing or Choice?* (Gregg Revivals 1993)

and *New Religious Movements: A Practical Introduction* (HMSO 1989, 5th impression 1995).

She is the founder of INFORM (Information Network Focus on Religious Movements), a charity supported by the British Government and mainstream Churches which offers enquirers information that is as accurate, balanced and up-to-date as possible about the new religions. She is the only non-American to have been elected President of the Society for the Scientific Study of Religion. Her current research interests are changes with the second generation in new religions, religion in Eastern Europe and the former Soviet Union, and the New Age; and the Armenian Diaspora and the Republic of Armenia.

Thomas Gandow

Thomas Gandow was born in Berlin, where he also received his theology degree. He worked as vicar to a Korean congregation in Berlin and for the 'Berliner Missionswerk' before becoming minister in Berlin-Zehlendorf in 1985. Since 1978, he was 'Beauftragter für Neue Religiöse Gemeinschaften' in the 'Jugendpfarramt' for West Berlin; following the reunification of Germany in 1992, he became Commissioner for Issues of Sects and Ideologies within the Evangelische Kirche of Berlin-Brandenburg. He is director of the Berlin-based 'Archiv für Religions — und Weltanschauungs fragen Berlin', an Institute for the scientific research of religions in Europe, specializing in Germany and Eastern Europe. Since 1995, he has been editor of the journal *Berliner Dialog: Informationen und Standpunkte zur Religiösen Begegnung*.

Michael Rupprecht Garde

Michael Garde was born in South Africa but has lived in Ireland since the age of 12. He started his career in Hotel Management but changed to studying theology. 1968-1969: Oar Hill Theological College (Anglican). 1969-1970: L'Abri, Switzerland (Reformed). 1970-1973: The Irish Baptist College, Belfast, Ireland. 1973: Diploma in Theology at London University, England. 1973-1975: Bachelor of Divinity at Pontifical University, St. Patricks College, Maynooth, Ireland. 1975-1976: Higher Diploma in Education. 1992: Clinical Pastoral Education (CPE) the Mater Hospital, Dublin, Ireland. He worked with the Mennonite Church in Ireland from 1975-1995. His initial contact with the Dialogue Centre was through the WSCF

Conference in Cardiff, Wales in 1979, and since through the December seminars in Denmark. Since 1992 Mike Garde has been the Field Worker of the Dialogue Centre in Ireland. This is an ecumenical venture representing the four mainline denominations - the Roman Catholic Church, the Church of Ireland, the Presbyterian Church and the Methodist Church. He hopes to publish a book on NRMs in Ireland in late 1997.

Teresa Gonçalves.
Teresa Gonçalves holds a degree in Romance Languages from the University of Coimbra, Portugal, and an MA in Religious Sciences from the Gregorian University, Rome. She is in charge of the topic 'New Religious Movements' in the Pontifical Council for Interreligious Dialogue.

Massimo Introvigne
Massimo Introvigne holds degrees from the Pontifical Gregorian University in Rome (BA in Philosophy) and from the University of Turin (Law Doctorate, with a major in Philosophy and Sociology of Law). Besides practising law as a partner in one of Italy's largest firm, he has been a part-time professor of Sociology of Religion at the Southern University of Theology and is currently a professor in the Faculty of Theology, lecturing in History and Sociology of Religious Movements at Queen of the Apostles University in Rome. He is the author or editor of twenty books in the field of new religious movements and contemporary magic (in Italian, some of them translated into French and German), and of more than one hundred scholarly articles. From 1988 he is the Director of CESNUR, the Centre for Studies on New Religions, a post-graduate research facility and a network of scholars of new religious movements headquartered in Torino, Italy, and sponsored by the rightwing Catholic organization *Alleanza Catholica.*

Reender Kranenborg
Dr Reender Kranenborg is research-professor at the Faculty of Theology of the Vrije Universiteit in Amsterdam, department for Religious Studies. His study regards the modern religiosity in the west in the widest sense (new religious movements, esoterism, new age etc.). He is the editor of *Religieuze Bewegingen in Nederland* (Religious Movements in the Netherlands), which is published

twice a year. He has written many books on this subject; his thesis *Zelfverwerkelijking* (on eastern movements in the west), and books on reincarnation and about the difficult relationship of New Age and the Christian faith. He is also working as a minister of the Reformed Church of Amsterdam).

Jean-François Mayer

Jean-François Mayer earned a doctoral degree in history at the University of Lyons (France) in 1984 with a thesis about the Swedenborgian movement in French-speaking Switzerland. From 1987 to 1990, he conducted an historical and sociological research about new religious movements in Switzerland on behalf of the Swiss National Fund for Scientific Research. Since 1991 he has been active in a new field security policy, and is currently working at the Swiss Central Office for General Defense.

He published his first book about NRMs in 1985. Among his books published in the 90s: *Confessions d'un chasseur de sectes* (Paris: Cerf, 1990), *Les nouvelles voies spirituelles. Enquête sur la religiosité parallèle en Suisse* (Lausanne: L'Age d'Homme, 1993) and *Mit Sekten konfrontiert* (Freiburg: Paulusverlag, 1995). He is also the co-editor of a series of introductory books about religious topics, published by the Editions du Cerf (Paris) and the Editions Fides (Montréal).

J. Gordon Melton

J. Gordon Melton, the Director of the Institute for the Study of American Religion, Santa Barbara, California, was born and raised in Birmingham, Alabama. He graduated from Birmingham-Southern College (BA, 1964), Garrett Theological Seminary (MDiv, 1968) and Northwestern University (Ph.D., History and Literature of Religions, 1975). In 1968 he was ordained an elder in the United Methodist Church. He has pastored churches in Indiana and Illinois.

In 1969 Dr Melton founded the Institute for the Study of American Religion, a research facility focusing on the study of America's many religious groups and organizations, especially the many small and nonconventional religions. The first major products of the Institute were the *Directory of Religious Bodies in the United States* (1978, second edition, 1992) and the *Encyclopedia of American Religions* (1979, fourth edition, 1992), now a standard reference book on North American religious bodies. Founded in Evanston, Illinois, the institute moved to Santa Barbara in 1985, and Melton subsequently was named research specialist with the Department of Religious Studies of the University of California, Santa Barbara.

Since the appearance of the *Encyclopedia of American Religions* in 1979, Dr Melton has authored som twenty-five books including *The Cult Experience* (1982), the *Biographical Dictionary of Cult and Sect Leaders* (1986) and the *Encyclopedia of African-American Religion* (1993). He is a member of the committee on New Religious Study Area of the American Academy of Religion and is the immediate past president of the Communal Studies Association. He is also a member of the Society for the Scientific Study of Religion.

Ole Riis

Since 1985 has been Associate Professor of Sociology of Religion at the Theological Faculty of the University of Aarhus, attached to the non-confessional department of the study of religion. Member of the Board of the Danish Sociological Association, and member of the Board of the International Society for the Sociology of Religion.

Research publications include approximately one hundred items in Danish, about thirty items in English, two in Italian, one in Spanish and one in French. The topics mainly concern the methodology of social science and the sociology of religion. His most widely known book in Denmark (written in cooperation with Professor P. Gundelach), concerns values among Danes today, *Danskernes Vaerdier*, Forlaget Sociology, Copenhagen 1992. This Danish project has now been expanded into a Scandinavian one, and presented in a publication,*Scandinavian Values*, Uppsala University 1994 (co-edited with Professor T. Petterson), Uppsala. His most recent book in Danish is *Metoder og Teorier i Religionssociologien* which describes the methodological and theoretical guidelines for working as a sociologist of religion. He is involved in several international projects concerning value pluralism and value transformation, and is at present working on an interdisciplinary study of religious pluralism in the Nordic countries. Furthermore he is involved in a project on religious and moral pluralism in Western Europe.

Friederike Valentin
Friederike Valentin was born in 1949 in Vienna, Austria. She studied Roman Catholic Theology and took her doctorate at Vienna University in 1975. Since 1971 Dr Valentin has been head of the *Referat für Weltanschauungsfragen* in Vienna, which works on a cross-regional basis in Austria.

Together with Hans Gasper, Bonn, and Joachim Müller, Balgach in Switzerland, she edits the *Lexikon der Sekten, Sondergruppen und Weltanschauungen,* (Freiburg: Herder).

Together with Hans Gasper, Bonn, she also edits the series *Sekten, Sondergruppen und Weltanschauungen,* (Freiburg: Herder).

Index